Tales From Under The Moon Roof:

Stories of a Globe-Trotting Uber Driver

Tales From Under The Moon Roof:

Stories of a Globe-Trotting Uber Driver

LOUISE COOK

TALES FROM UNDER THE MOON ROOF:
Stories of a Globe-Trotting Uber Driver

Manufactured in the United States of America
First printing August 2015

ISBN-13: 978-0-9966359-1-2
ISBN: 0996635912

Library of Congress Number: 2015912682

DEDICATION

For my family and friends

ACKNOWLEDGMENTS

Just like every author, I struggle in crediting the many people who have shared their stories, given me guidance as I wrote, and provided images that bring the stories to life. Telling good stories is an art form, shaped by education and experience. My parents, Billy and Elizabeth Cook, sacrificed so that I could go to an excellent college, assuring that I would be able to write and both have many stories to tell.

Talking with Uber clients has created a new chapter in my life—one that challenges me to find that singular story each of my passengers has. Without Uber clients, this book would not exist.

The members of the Decatur Writers Collaborative provide support, knowledge, and criticism. Nancy stepped in to create a well-designed cover. Sukru and Minh keep my computers going. Precious keeps me entertained and loved. Harry Campbell, The Ride Share Guy, keeps me up to date on the business of ride-sharing. KT Ashely has helped throughout the publishing process, advising and making me laugh. The Earwood family are great storytellers whom I draw on for inspiration.

My husband, Joe, and my son, Alex, are my touchstones.

INTRODUCTION

When Uber came to Atlanta in April 2014, I thought it might be a way to earn a little extra money. Driving, however, I realized what interested me most was the conversations I had with riders—even those that had consumed way too many adult beverages. I might pick up a well-known rap artist one shift or someone of very modest means who had created a charity for young girls. I never knew. However, there are few occupations that could provide such a diverse clientele.

I blog about clients and other people I meet. My Uber passengers form the core of my writing, but I have branched out to include topical issues, humor, travel, and human interest stories.

My husband and I like to travel, taking what we call "Louise and Joe's Big Adventures." No matter our commitment to relax, our trips always become "forced fun." On the go from morning to night, we seize every opportunity to explore and learn. In the last few years we have been to Italy, England, France, Monaco, and Russia. Story ideas often flow from the people I meet in other countries.

I hope you enjoy my adventures. For more, subscribe to my blog:
www.talesfromunderthemoonroof.com

TABLE OF CONTENTS

Chapter 1
The Assassin's Throne

One of the most deadly killers on the planet lurks in bathrooms but almost no one talks about it, even in whispers. It just sits there, silently waiting. Can you guess what it is? I talked to my friends at CDC, I searched the internet, and I wasn't surprised to learn that germs and bacteria lurk in bathrooms. The experts at CDC said you can avoid most of those by practicing proper hygiene and cleaning bathrooms regularly.

The bathroom is also cited by many people as "the most dangerous room in a home," largely because of the risk of falls on slick surfaces. I took a poll of friends and they said that the toilet is probably the most dangerous fixture in the bathroom, but their rationale was based on the possibility of catching a disease, particularly in a public bathroom.

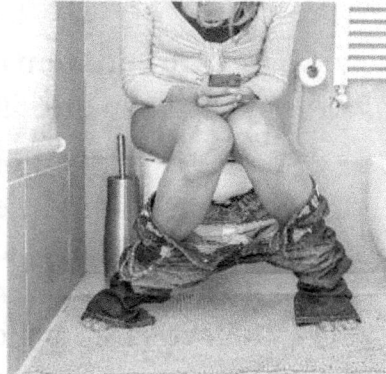

The aptly-named, Porcelain Goddess, is probably the number one killer of cell phones all over the world. Toilets are like the Sirens of Greek mythology that lured sailors to their deaths with their enchanted, but deadly, songs.

I learned this the hard way, by dropping my cell phone, not once, but twice, into a toilet this past weekend at the Master's Tournament in Augusta, Georgia. Juggling my purse and my cell phone, I went into the stall, used the toilet, and noticed that the roll was empty.

Being a nice person, I decided to put a new roll onto the holder. The problem was that the new toilet paper was sitting in a basket on the back of the toilet, so when turning around to get it, my phone heard the siren call and leapt out of my hands and into the depths. Here I was, about to end a financially lucrative day by driving two people to and from the Masters Golf Tournament in Augusta, when the killer struck.

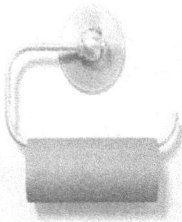

"S***, s***, s***." I exclaimed. I tried to think of options to get it out. I couldn't go out and say to the receptionist, "Excuse me, but do you have some long tongs, or maybe one of those 'pick-up devices' they advertise for older people? You see, I've dropped my cell phone into the toilet." In the end, I fished it out with my hands. *Please, please, please let it work*, I prayed. *I have insurance, but I'll still have to pay and I'm not due for an upgrade yet. How will I navigate back to Atlanta with no phone?* All of this ran through my head as I got the phone and dried it off as best I could.

Pressing the on button did not produce the desired effect. While still kneeling on the floor, fooling with the phone, trying to get it to power up, I dropped it again. This time the expletives and self-deprecating thoughts were worse. *How could I possibly do something so stupid? I can never go into the Verizon store and tell them I dropped the phone into a toilet. I could just imagine their disgust and unwillingness to touch the phone. They probably have a special crew, dressed in haz mat suits that come out to take the phone away. I'm going to lose an entire day dealing with getting a new phone. I'll have to say that I dropped it into the sink, not the toilet.*

I put the new roll of toilet paper on, and washed my hands and the phone thoroughly.

I went out to the lobby and desperately searched the internet for a fast solution. Vacuum chambers, rice, cat litter, and other suggestions offered little hope. *Oh, yeah,* I mocked silently, *everybody has a spare vacuum chamber lying around.* Fortunately, one of my passengers had Google maps, and we headed back to Atlanta.

Arriving at home, I put the phone in a box and rigged my hair dryer to create a "drying chamber." Still nothing. The next morning, it still wouldn't power on. *Dammit, dammit, dammit, I had to go to Verizon—it was inevitable.*

My phone was just two months away from an upgrade so I went to one of their stores to see what I could do. I won't belabor you with all the details, but it was the nightmare I expected. However, a new phone arrived at my door on Tuesday morning.

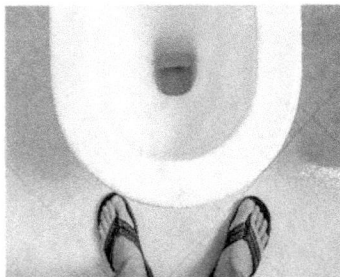

George, a new friend of mine, admitted that he has lost three phones when he gets up early in the morning, stumbles sleepily into the bathroom, and checks his email while relieving himself. He managed to dry one out and save it, but the other two were toast.

This woman, who obviously was angry at her boyfriend, put all of his electronic devices in the toilet. I have no first-hand account of this, but I think this is the ultimate breakup revenge. Unfortunately, my husband is too nice for me to take this kind of action, and even worse, he's not as plugged-in as I am and would probably be happy to be freed of 24/7 communication. In fact, he always denies getting my texts and phone calls. *Hmmmm...He's had three carriers and had the same problems with each one.* You think it could be that he's avoiding me?

All of this leads me to the question, "How many people actually admit to dropping their phones into a toilet. I mean, really. Who's going to walk into a store or call customer support and admit this?"

That's why toilets are the silent killers. It's probably an epidemic. I think I'll call my CDC friends again.

Chapter 2
The Body Bag

In my family, our parting questions before a trip were always the same. "Well, if anything happens, you know what to do, don't you?"

"Yes," we'd respond, "Just get a body bag until you get back." This may seem harsh, but our philosophy was that if someone had died, there was nothing to be done, so you might as well enjoy your trip and have the service when you got home.

We have many good storytellers in my family, none better than my parents, Billy and Elizabeth Cook; and the Earwoods, all of whom had a gene that was activated by the sound of a fast car.

BILLY, LOUISE, JOE HALE AND ELIZABETH

Many stories tend to become embellished, getting better with each retelling. Most are behind-the-scene stories about drag and sports car racing. Talking at 200 mph (his normal speed), Terry

Earwood says, "The stories are true; they are not the creation of some reality show writer. You cain't make up stuff like this."

The incident described here happened about 1973, when laws and regulations were more lax. Tommy Wilson was an airplane mechanic at Peachtree DeKalb Airport, who in earlier years had raced motorcycles.

He walked with a limp and there was hardly a body part not held together with screws or pins. Baker Motor Company sponsored several race cars that were stored in a hangar at the airport where Wilson worked. There was nothing Wilson couldn't fix, and he started helping with the two Chevrons shown below.

He was an excellent mechanic and was soon hired to work on all of the race cars. He was a colorful character (one of many) with whom we spent many happy hours at racetracks (or on the back of his motorcycle).

As my father, Billy Cook, tells it, "Tommy was a lean, lanky, good 'ole Georgia boy, about 5'10. He was a chain-smoker whose nails were yellow and usually stained by grease. He liked beer, 'but he would drink anything that wouldn't burn his lips.' He always wore navy blue coveralls when he was working."

In the 1960s and the early 1970s, the racing community in Atlanta was fairly small and there was a lot of overlap. Championship MOPAR* drag racer, Bill Tanner, shared a repair shop in Doraville with Hugh Don Smith, a sports car mechanic. Tom Wilson would often stop by the garage, and that's how he met Tanner and Terry Earwood, (at right), who was a winning drag racer first in Tanner's cars and then with Steve Bagwell (above).

Knowing Wilson at the time, I can attest to the core of this story that explains my family's ritual when someone travelled.

As Earwood tells it, *"Wilson's dad, whom he hadn't seen in forever, passed away peacefully in his sleep on a cot:*

In the rear of small used car lot in McDonough, Georgia, about an hour south of Atlanta. After work that day, Wilson stopped by the repair shop on his way down to McDonough and informed Hugh Don and Bill that he was finally gonna' see his dad after all these years, but left out the little detail of the 'passing.'"

Wilson slept in the car until the funeral home opened the next morning. Neither Wilson nor his dad had any money, so the McDonough funeral director suggested he send his dad's body on Southern Railway to South Carolina in a plain pine box. "Listen mistah," Tommy replied, "I ain't got no money. Is there some way you could hep me out? Let me jest do this one last thing for my daddy."

"Weelll...I guess we could git you a permit to transport the body to South Carolina, have you got a car or somethin' we could put him in if we put him in a body bag rather than a coffin? We need to move fast, though, 'cause pretty soon he ain't gonna be that easy to bend."

"Oh, yeah, that ain't no problem. I can git him there," Wilson replied.

"Alright, son, I'll get stahted on the permit. It might take a while, though."

Late that afternoon, when the permit was approved, the funeral home director told Wilson to bring his car around to the back and they would help him get his dad's body in the car. Wilson had neglected to tell him that he was driving a small, two-seater MGB like the one here.

When the funeral director saw the car, all of the color leeched from his face, making him look like he had been embalmed as well. At that point, however, he would have done almost anything to get Wilson and his daddy out of his sight, so they lowered the convertible top and wrangled the body into the passenger seat.

Earwood picks up the story again:

"When Wilson got back to Atlanta, he walked into Tanner's shop and asked Smith and Tanner if they'd like to see his dad, who was out in his car, and could they maybe help get him out of the car.... A bit curious as to why his dad couldn't get out on his own, they stopped what they were doing and followed Wilson to the parking lot. Much to their surprise, the late Mr. Wilson was, even tho' 'upright' in the passenger seat, where he had sorta 'stiffened up,' he was at least fully enclosed in a body bag for his final trip home."

Tommy had mainly stopped at the repair shop to ask a coupla' favors He needed a night's rest before the trek to South Carolina, so would they possibly let his Dad spend his last night in Georgia inside the shop, maybe on a workbench--to maybe 'stretch out,' no pun intended, instead of 'couped up' in the tiny sports car. And could he maybe borrow Tanner's new Dodge truck to further continue his Dad's 'reposturing,' by 'stretching him out in the back' for the remainder of the trip.

Tanner said they had to lower the top of the MG to get Mr. Wilson out, and, even tho' decades before social media, they still drew a pretty big crowd to see their overnight guest at Doraville Sports Car Repair. Tanner also reported that every time he worked on that one bench after that, he felt 'someone was watching him!' But he had always been a little paranoid, so who knows...."

Wilson left the next morning in Tanner's new Dodge pickup heading for South Carolina. The place and manner of interment of his daddy is unknown. Neither Mr. Wilson nor the body bag, however, were in the back when the truck was returned to Tanner the following day.

*The acronym MOPAR refers to cars built by Chrysler, primarily Dodges and Plymouths. However, to most auto enthusiasts, the term refers to the high performance division of the company that produced muscle cars such as the Dodge Charger and the Plymouth Barracuda.

Chapter 3
Across Continents and Years: Sudan

I have found so many intersections between my passengers and me that I can almost always find common ground. In this case, the convergence of two people from opposite sides of the globe started in 1995, almost 20 years ago. Each of us had been to many parts of the world but our paths had not crossed until an Uber ride that started in Midtown Atlanta.

I picked up two guys and one of my first questions was, "So, where you guys from?"

I thought I picked up an African accent from one. He said he had lived all over the place, the U.S., Asia, and so forth. I don't usually push people, but curiosity prevailed.

"Where did you grow up," I asked.

"Sudan."

"North or South? "

"North."

"Were you there in 1995 by any chance?"

"Yes, I was."

"Do you remember if you got vaccinated that year?"

"Yes, I certainly did and ever since then I have been afraid of needles. In fact, I punched out the next doctor who tried to stick me. I was a big football player at Ohio, and I was not about to get a shot. I am terrified of needles to this day."

He was incredulous. "How could you possibly know this," he asked.

"Well, I have to tell you a story," I said. "In 1995, I was working at The Carter Center when former President Jimmy Carter, his staff, and many others negotiated a cease-fire between North and South Sudan to allow health workers to reach children and adults at risk of a number of preventable diseases like polio, mumps, measles, and many others. Health workers were sent from every agency that could help, and international teams were quickly set up in Khartoum, in North Sudan, and Lokochogio, Kenya (to serve South Sudan). It was everyone's hope that the cease-fire could be extended if Sudanese leaders on both sides of the conflict could see the benefits of saving children's lives.

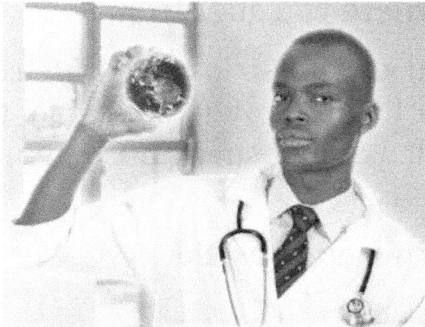

Another agenda was to prolong peace talks between the warring factions in the hope of a negotiated peace. "

"Yes," he said, the fighting was terrible. My parents left the country, in fact. Did you go to Sudan?"

"No, I played a very small role in the effort, but it's been one of my proudest moments in my life. Every day, I called the Khartoum and the Lokochogio offices to get precise information about what had been accomplished that day: numbers of children vaccinated, number of adults treated, and other measurements of the program's success.

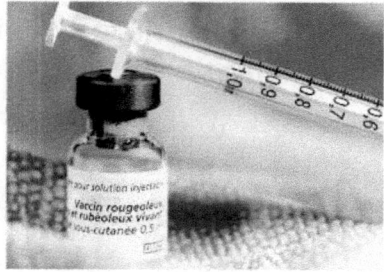

President Carter wanted nothing short of reaching every possible person as quickly as possible, and the aid agencies were scrambling to collaborate to make this happen. It was my job to write a daily report that summarized actions and also detailed where aid workers needed access the following day. There was always the danger that planes landing on dirt airstrips in the middle of a war zone, would be shot down."

A few moments passed in silence. Suddenly, this large black man reached completely around my seat, and pulled me into a deep hug. Both of us were teary-eyed. We had reached his destination and said goodbye. He turned back to the car, however, and reached through my window, and pulled me into another huge hug. "Thank you," he said, and then ran to catch up with his friend.

Update: Wikpedia says that there are around forty-nine aid agencies still located in Lokochogio as well as a large orthopedic hospital that serves the country of South Sudan.[1]

The war between North and South ended in 2005, but there are so many factions fighting in the area that one of the largest refugee camps in the region is but a short distance from Lokichogio.

If you want to help, you can find more information or make a donation to The Carter Center, Doctors Without Borders, UNICEF, Norwegian Church Aid Act Alliance, or many other organizations. Norway has always been active in war-torn areas, and from Kenya, they work primarily in the Darfur Region of South Sudan, where they estimate 390,000 people have been displaced in the first seven months of this year.

---

[1]*Wikipedia*. https://en.wikipedia.org/wiki. Accessed 8/17/15.

Chapter 4
A Clash of Cultures:
A Saudi Arabian Man's Fear

Living near Emory University, where almost all of the students use Uber, I'm always pleased when I drive a student who's at the Rollins School of Public Health because I spent my happiest days when working in public health. In one day alone, I drove four from the school, a young woman from China and two women from Boston. The fourth was one of my most memorable clients, a young man from the Kingdom of Saudi Arabia whom I met at the start of the school year.

Ahmed, who had only been in the U.S. for three days, told me that he was terrified to go out because he had heard that people could carry guns, and that this spring, in Georgia, they would be able to carry concealed weapons. He had also heard another student talking about being held up at an ATM in downtown Atlanta. Another Uber client, a Saudi Arabian woman who goes to school in Atlanta, told me," It's no wonder Ahmed was frightened. We are led to believe that the U.S. is a very violent country where few are safe. We see

violence on American television shows and [people] think that truly reflects what the U.S. is like."

It was a short ride to his destination so I stopped the fare when we arrived and talked with him for a few minutes. He was incredulous that this would be permitted and he was terrified that he would be shot in a public building like a supermarket or at the school.

Having no simple way of explaining such a complex issue, I could only reassure him that his likelihood of being shot was infinitesimal. I advised him to take reasonable safety measures when going out to clubs or ATMs late at night, however. "Just take along a friend," I suggested.

Not knowing how prescient my words would become, I went on to say that race and culture were major factors in gun violence and that, with his fair skin, he could easily pass as a "white American." I tried to explain the significance of this but I knew that I had fallen short. However, recent events in the U.S. have certainly brought this issue into the spotlight, particularly when police are involved.

Ahmed wanted to know more about American policy on gun control, so I touched briefly on how Constitutional guarantees, powerful lobbying groups, and personal opinion have shaped policy. I gave him a very short overview but, like many issues, it could not be explained effectively in just a few minutes, particularly to someone from such a different culture and system of laws.

Later, our conversation made me want to know how our two countries differed in this area. Researchers who compile data about gun policy, estimate that homicides (by any method) in the U.S. is about 4.7 per 100,000 people while in Saudi Arabia it is only 2.7 per 100,000.[2] They also found that while there are about 300,000,000 guns in private ownership in the U.S, there are only about 6,000,000, in Saudi Arabia.[3] In a comparison of the *rate* of private gun ownership in 178 countries, Saudi Arabia ranked number seven, after Yemen, Switzerland, Finland, Serbia, and Cyprus.[4]

It is difficult to obtain statistics from closed societies. However, Susie of Arabia, an American who lives in Jeddah, has been writing about the

---

[2] Alpers, Philip and Marcus Wilson. 2014. *Guns in Saudi Arabia: Rate of Homicide per 100,000 People* (any method). Sydney School of Public Health, The University of Sydney GunPolicy.org, 16 July. http://bit.ly/1KuL7er Accessed 5/9/2015

[3] Ibid.

[4] Ibid. NOTE: Small Arms Survey calculates guns per 100 people and total civilian guns by averaging numbers reported from various sources. Most recent data is from 2007. UNODC's homicide data is from 2010 and 2009, depending on the country. SOURCE: UNODC, Small Arms Survey, Guardian Datablog.

country since 2007. She told me, "While handguns and hunting rifles are sold, it's rare to read about crimes committed here using guns of any kind. Traditionally, men in smaller villages bring rifles to weddings and fire them...which can have disastrous results."[5] What she is referring to is the accidental death or injury that occurs when bullets fired randomly hit other wedding guests.

In a more recent story, Al Jazeerah[6] reported that Saudi Arabia had now banned such celebrations as a result of a 2012 incident that killed 25 women and children, and injured 30 more. A power line fell on a metal door, electrocuting the women and children as they tried to escape through the only door.

I was surprised to learn that gun ownership in the U.S. has actually declined every decade since the 1970s. The New York Times used data from the General Social Survey, which has been conducting polls since 1973,[7] to conclude, "The household gun ownership rate has fallen from an average of 50 percent in the 1970s, to 49 percent

---

[5] Susie of Arabia. *Jeddah: Rifle Shop and Gun Control.* http://bit.ly/1JWPqlK Accessed 5/9/2015.

[6] Aljazerah. *Blaze kills Saudi Arabia wedding guests.* http://bit.ly/1H5qg0G Accessed 5/9/2015.

[7] The General Social Survey is a government-funded program funded by the National Science Foundation and conducted at the University of Chicago. The most The most recent study, from 2012, may be found at http://www3.norc.org/gss+website/ Accessed 5/9/2015.

in the 1980s, 43 percent in the 1990s and 35 percent in the 2000s."[8]

Another surprising finding was that while "...gun ownership remains widespread...a smaller percentage of gun owners possess an increasing percentage of the gun stock." In other words, people who don't already own guns are not buying them. A 2004 Gallup Poll concluded that personal safety is cited as the number one reason people own guns, not the second amendment's "right to bear arms," that is often touted by pro-gun organizations. The NRA estimates that there are more than 2 million self-defense shootings every year. The organization actively promotes gun ownership for personal safety.

A study by the Violence Policy Center concluded that guns are rarely used to kill criminals or stop crimes. It went on to state that in 2010, across the nation, there were only 230 justifiable homicides involving a private citizen using a firearm reported to the Federal Bureau of Investigation's Uniform Crime Reporting (UCR) Program.

In 2007, the New York Police Department commissioned the Rand Corporation to conduct the effectiveness of its gun training for police officers. In part, the report found the following:

---

[8] *New York Times. Share of Homes With Guns Shows 4-Decade Decline.* http://nyti.ms/1nQGgrQ Accessed 1/3/2015.

"...during 2006, only 156 Officers out of the force of some 37,000, were involved in a firearm-discharge incident. Fewer than half of those incidents involved an officer shooting at a human being. Most involved police shooting at dogs. The average hit rate for NYPD Officers involved in a gunfight between 1998 and 2006 was 18 percent. For every five shots, four bullets missed the intended target and went somewhere else. And that hit rate is consistent with the "normal" hit rate in armed encounters which hasn't changed much for years and years."[9]

This study and others point out that while we can train people to use guns safely in controlled conditions, the reality is that this training does not transfer into real-life situations when people are confronted by armed violence directed at them. Even with training, New York officers were only able to hit the target 18% of the time.

If we arm school teachers, bus drivers, and others where kids and adults are congregated, what is the likelihood that innocent bystanders would be hit? After all, the other four bullets that don't hit the target have to go somewhere. Seems to me that it's just like the villagers in Saudi Arabia, who kill or maim wedding-goers.

---

[9] The Rand Corporation, 2008. The Rand Corp. *Study of NYPD Handgun Training.* http://pointshooting.com/1arand.htm Accessed 31 December 2014.

Chapter 5

My First Time in the Back Seat

It was my first time, and how many times had I heard, "If you go out to bars and pick up men, you need to take protection." I picked up an Uber client who wanted something from me and neither of us had what we needed. Of course we didn't discover that until we were at the point of no return. It all happened in the back seat of my car. Fortunately, I was able to pull the car off the road in time.

But let me start at the beginning. About 1 AM, I got an Uber call to pick up a group from a bar in Virginia-Highlands. Two women and a man quickly got in the car and I started to pull away. But one woman screamed, "Stop, we have to wait for 'Bob.' There he comes, right now," and pointed out the windshield. "Can you believe he got kicked out of the bar just because he was dancing with the bartender's girlfriend," she asked.

From my perspective I saw a bar manager guiding a very drunk 'Bob' toward the car. Fortunately, they made room for 'Bob' in the back seat and one of the women moved to the front. She kept repeating that 'Bob' had been thrown out due to the bartender's girlfriend, however, I knew he had been thrown out before he passed out.

'Bob' was incoherent and kept falling over onto the lap of the woman in the back seat. She kept trying to get him upright with little success. Then she decided that she wanted to find out how big his penis was. Over and over, she said, "You know, I'll bet you have a really small penis. Let's find out." She also kept asking him if he was all right. I didn't know if she was unzipping his pants or what. My focus was on driving and I knew that they were all inebriated and therefore they needed to be out of my car as soon as possible. (My husband, Joe, later volunteered that all men's testicles shrink when they drink.)

All of a sudden, I heard, "Pull over," from the backseat. Oh no, I knew I was unprepared and that 'Bob' was about to throw up in my car. I was desperate to keep my new car clean, and fortunately, I was able to pull over in time for 'Bob' to open the door and throw up outside. I had been very lucky.

I was telling the story to a friend, and he said that when his daughter was the "designated driver" in her sorority, she carried a bucket and sponge in her car. "If any of that gets on your upholstery, you can never get the smell out," he said. At that point, I knew exactly how to protect myself in the future: a bucket, disinfectant, paper towels, and a sponge!

Chapter 6

Using Uber in Moscow, Russia

We had been warned about the pitfalls of using taxis in Russia. So, as an Uber driver in Atlanta, I was excited about using the service in Russia when we visited last year. They don't have UberX, but they have Black Cars, typically Mercedes or BMWs. The first day we were in Moscow there was nothing planned, so I pressed the Uber icon on the phone and in about 20 minutes, a black Mercedes picked me up. The driver didn't speak any English, but I had a Russian/English map, and I was going to Red Square, so everything went smoothly.

While I did get chased off by a security guard because (as I later learned), I was at the entrance to the Kremlin where Russian President Vladimir Putin's office is, I got the same driver for the return trip.

Not having been in the country more than 12 hours, I was anxious to learn how much access to smartphones and other forms of

communications Russians have with the outside world. I pulled out my smartphone, and showed the driver some pictures from Amazon.com, trying to ascertain whether they could buy things online. I guess my big mistake was streaming an episode of *The Sopranos*.

Suddenly the driver pulled over, dialed a number, spoke a lot of Russian, and finally handed the phone to me. The person on the other end spoke some English and wanted to know where I wanted to go, saying that the driver was confused. I guess the driver thought I wanted to shop for a gun; I don't know. It took quite a while to explain that no, I just wanted to go back to the ship. We went back and forth between the driver, the English translator, and me for several minutes, but finally we took off and I made it back to the ship. The driver was extremely nice.

Unfortunately, the next two days did not go well at all. I was robbed of $450 by one of the drivers, and even though we had maps and the location of our ship written out in Russian, the next day's driver took 90 minutes for a 30 minute trip because he couldn't find the location. I even had the phone numbers for the ship, but he swore that no one answered. We stopped at least three times for him to get directions, and he both took money from my wallet and doubled-billed me. Uber Moscow later assured me that he had been fired, but would not give me his full name and license plate number so that I could file a police report.

I finally figured out that Uber is relatively new to Russia and that the GPS systems used to locate passengers and locations is not as sophisticated, so you have to make sure that you check to assure that you put the "pin" on exactly where you are. I don't think the drivers are all that familiar with using maps and locations in the city, either.

One nice young man took us on a 30 minute trip to go 1 Km. He finally admitted that he had just moved from Siberia and he thought that a pedestrian mall, a big blue rectangle on our map, was a river. Each time we used Uber we had to ask a Russian tourist on the street to talk to the drivers in Russian, or we had to be switched to a dispatcher who spoke "some" English.

Chapter 7
Don't Touch That Dial

Usually, I get one of several questions from clients about my car or driving for Uber:

Are you ever afraid?

Wow, is this YOUR car?

Did you buy it like this?

Are you putting me on?

Whoa, look at this moon/sun roof.

What kind of car is this?

I'll bet you have some crazy stories.

Who were your worst clients?

Who were your most memorable clients?

So, what's the name of your blog?

What do you like most/least about driving for Uber?

I can easily answer the first one. No, I've never been afraid while driving for Uber. The only time I've ever been a little uncomfortable, and I go all over the city at all times of the day and night, and sometimes I know I'm the only white woman in a mile radius, is when I was

on a two-block street that was clearly a place where selling/buying drugs was the ONLY reason to go down the street. Even then, once faced with the reality, I just waved to everyone hanging out on the street, and moved on, while frantically calling my clients to get a better address.

Of course, I've been robbed at gunpoint, and a couple of years ago, I drove a golf cart through a Hell's Angels encampment (having gone in the back, unmarked side) by mistake. With the Hell's Angels, I just waved and kept moving. I later went back and bought a motorcycle jacket from one of them, and visited the booths of all the chapters in the "official" area. Personally, I think a good, old-fashioned wave (and not one of those from the elbow used by beauty queens) and a 5'1" high, old, white woman can defuse most situations. My father, Billy Cook, would both wave and bellow out, "Hey, how y'all doin'?" However, I digress.

To get back to Uber, I can easily say that the thing I most like about it is my clients. I have met some of the most interesting, hilarious, and fascinating people that I would never have met otherwise. And they are all potential fodder for this blog. The second thing I like about driving for Uber is talking, and Uber clients, most of whom could be my grandchildren, are polite listeners. Many are unaccustomed to seeing 60+ years' old women driving around late at night and feel that they should be polite; still others find me funny or infect me with their humor.

However, there are a small number of Uber riders who really irritate me. Last fall, I picked up some Georgia Tech students, the same clients who had sent me down the "drug street." I had circled another block a couple of times when I finally found them in a gravel alleyway that passed as a street. They were incredulous that I hadn't seen them, up on the roof, waving to me. (After all, if you're looking for a street address, isn't that where most people would look?) They had had a few adult beverages in preparation for going downtown to the Outkast concert and they immediately started in with questions.

"Who were your worst riders, ever" they enquired.

I thought for a seconds, then responded, "You know, I drove my worst Uber clients just this afternoon."

"Whoa, what did they do?

Well, I picked up these three women from Emory, and they were going to have high tea at Dr. Bombay's Underwater Tea Shop, whose owner, Katrell Christie-Tit, I have written about. Afterwards, they were getting their nails done. None of them were interested in the charity supported by Katrell's shop through monthly dinners, used book sales, and a variety of fund-

raising activities. But that wasn't what annoyed me most.

"So, what happened?"

"The one who sat up front really pissed me off," I said. "The first thing she did was start changing radio stations."

Not one, but all four of the men, bent their arms up at the elbows, with their palms facing outward, backed up as far as they could, and exclaimed, "Whooooah, noooo waaaaay." Clearly they, too, thought it a major breach of etiquette.

"Yep, if she didn't like what she heard on one station, she kept changing them until she found one she liked. And she just kept doing it throughout the ride. You can listen to almost any music in my car, but you need to ask permission first."

"So, can we plug my iPod in and listen to Outkast?"

"Of course," I responded. We turned it up really loud, put all the windows down, sang, and rocked-out all the way to Centennial Olympic Park. Now those guys I liked.

Chapter 8
Anna Katrell Christie & The Learning Tea

She was like many of my Uber clients; she wanted to stop at a friend's house to pick her up. "A blow-off- steam night out with a friend," she said. She was taking Uber because she wanted to drink as much as she wanted. She said that she had just returned from India the day before, it had been very stressful, and she just wanted to get drunk with friends to relieve the stress.

Curious, I asked, "What were you doing in India."

"I was there for the elections."

Knowing that the 2014 elections were a pivotal point in that country's future, I began to ask more questions. "Are you a reporter? Why were you there? Where did you go in the country? How long were you there? Had you been before?" One question led to another.

Very meekly, she said, "I support a group of girls in Darjeeling, and I needed to go see them in person." She seemed hesitant at first, but when she began to talk about her project, I felt her passion as she spoke.

She had gone to India when she was younger, trying to find her way in the world. A friend was going and she decided to take a chance. "I really didn't know what I wanted to do with my life and I just felt rootless," she explained. She ended up in a small village outside Darjeeling where she taught crafts to help the women in the village make money.

"I met three girls, aged 16, who wanted a different life--one where they could continue school and gain some independence, get their own place to live." She had no idea how she would do it, but vowed to return in six months with enough money to fund their education and living costs.

I had opened a tea shop in Candler Park, and I put a glass vase on the counter, together with a note that explained the purpose and asked for contributions. By the end of six months, I had enough to return with the money."

She had not only fulfilled three girls' dreams, she had found her purpose.

I caught up with Katrell last fall and she and a co-author who accompanied her on her last trip had signed a book deal in support of her work in India. She was very proud of "her girls," all of whom are in school and live in safe homes managed by a house-mother. On a planned trip to India, she hoped to expand to another city.

This summer, after visiting her husband's hometown in Vietnam, she married her fiance, journalist Thanh Truong, in a fishing boat on the Mekong River.

For more information on The Learning Tea, visit their website or visit Dr. Bombay's Underwater Tea Shop in Candler Park.

Chapter 9
John Lewis: A True American Hero

March 7, 2015 marks the 50th anniversary of what came to be known as "Bloody Sunday." When the movie *Selma* came out a few months ago, I wrote a post about why I didn't think I would be able, to see the movie in a theater. That Sunday, marchers met to conduct a nonviolent and orderly march across the Edmund Pettis Bridge, in Selma. Many of the civil rights workers had been working with the local community to achieve African-American voting rights.

I talked briefly about my career at The King Center, where I was responsible for the papers of Dr. King, the Southern Christian Leadership Conference (SCLC) CORE, and many other individuals and organizations, including those of the Student Nonviolent Leadership Committee (SNCC). I was one of the first people, in many years, to read the memos, speeches, sermons, and other documents created during the course of the 1955-1968 civil rights movement and in some way, I felt a spiritual connection to these people I had never met.

Yesterday, while driving for Uber, I picked up a man at the Emory Goizueta Business School who was in a hurry to catch a flight back to Washington, DC. After I asked him what he did, probing him for a specific response, he confessed that he was Congressman John Lewis' Chief of Staff, Michael Collins. He was rushing back because the Congressman was planning to take a group to Selma the next day to commemorate the anniversary.

At that moment, I admitted to myself that my reluctance to see the movie was because I didn't want to be reminded of the brutality towards a young man whose courage and commitment led him down a path that day that he knew would likely result in a brutal beating by Alabama State Troopers. His name is John Lewis, now the Congressman from the Fifth District in Georgia in the U.S. House of Representatives.

At the time of the March, Lewis was a founding member and Executive Director of the largest student-led civil rights organization in the U. S. He was also on the board of the SCLC. Lewis had met Dr. King much earlier, in 1958, wanting King's help in transferring from the American Baptist Theological Seminary, in Nashville, to the all-white

Troy State University near where he had grown up.

Dr. King, who had earned a PhD from Boston University, knew the importance of education and not feeling that the time was right to integrate Troy State, had counseled Lewis to come back to him after he had finished school in Nashville. He and others helped Lewis financially, and promised to find a place for him where he could be effective in the struggle.

In the late 1950s, Nashville was home to many students eager to participate in the civil rights movement and they had adopted the Ghandian principle of nonviolent protest. There were sit-ins and other protests aimed at integrating lunch counters, movie theaters, and other businesses. Many of these students, including John Lewis, would go on to be prominent strategists in the civil rights movement, including the Freedom Rides of 1961. Many would subsequently move to Atlanta.

On Sunday, March 7, Lewis's organization, the Student Nonviolent Coordinating Committee (SNCC), had decided it was too dangerous to march that day. In fact, doctors and nurses had come into Selma prepared to treat the wounded, and marchers had practiced moves to protect their heads and other vulnerable parts of their bodies. Dr. King had begged off due to preaching commitments in Atlanta. Lewis, however, deeply

courageous and unwilling to back down from his commitment to the people of Selma, stepped to the head of the group of 600 to cross the bridge, along with Hosea Williams from the SCLC. Both knew that state troopers in helmets, wielding canisters of tear gas and riot clubs were waiting for the order to break up the march using violent force. Lewis, shown above, wearing the rain coat, was seriously hurt.

I knew that Mr. Collins probably needed to review emails and make phone calls, but I couldn't stop myself from pouring my heart out to him about my deep and abiding respect for the congressman. I told him briefly about seeing all the documents that Lewis had written or seen during his tenure at the helm of the largest student-led organization in the civil rights movement, the Student Nonviolent Coordinating Committee (SNCC), and getting to know him at a distance by reading his history.

I had met Lewis many times, but it was usually at public events, and there would be no reason for him to remember me. I couldn't stop myself from telling Mr. Collins how I felt. "Whenever I am asked whom I most respect or admire, the Congressman's name is always the first on the tip of my tongue. While there are many whose names I would add, Lewis rises to the top because he has devoted his entire life to public service, never seeking fame or fortune. He has represented people by rising through the hierarchy of the Congress to serve as the voice of fairness and justice for all. I am proud to have lived in his district for many years, and to have the honor of being able to vote for him.

Throughout his life, from the very beginning, he has never wavered from his core beliefs even when they led him to take unpopular action or to stand as the sole voice of reason in a highly-politicized environment. His courage, on that day in Selma, was unparalleled. He knew he might not be alive at the end of the day. I can't imagine what bravery that took."

When we arrived at the airport, Mr. Collins graciously offered his card, and said, "If you ever need anything, please feel free to give me a call." We shook hands and he ran for the plane.

The information contained in the story comes both from my own examination of archival documents and the sources listed below:

Garrow, David J., *Protest at Selma: Martin Luther King, Jr. and the Voting Rights Act of 1965* (Yale University Press, 1978)

Garrow, David J., *Bearing the Cross: Martin Luther King, Jr. and the Southern Christian Leadership Conference* (New York: William Morrow & Co., 1986)

Branch, Taylor, *America in the King Years* (New York: Simon & Schuster, 1988-2006)

Carson, Clayborne, *In Struggle: SNCC and the Black Awakening of the 1960s* (Harvard University Press, 1995)

Chapter 10
Cupid's Undie Run with the Pattersons

I met Mike and Kathryn Patterson on Saturday night, Valentine's Day, taking them first to a restaurant in Smyrna, **On the Bayou**, for po-boys to take to a Mardi Gras party. Mike, in particular, raved about the restaurant. He said, "They get their bread directly from N'awlins. We can get you one. Are you sure you don't want a shrimp po-boy? We can call it in."

"No, thanks. I had a late lunch. I appreciate the offer though." We had a long drive and we chatted about their marriage last July. They were planning a short stay in Charleston, South Carolina.

I was complaining about traffic in Buckhead that afternoon, and Kathryn said, "Oh, I'll bet that was because of the Cupid's Undies Fun Run. We ran in it and had a great time. Of course we had few drinks before we ran because the start is in a bar. Then we had several drinks at the end. Oh my God, it was such fun."

She went on to tell me a little about the run, which benefits the **Children's Tumor Foundation**. The group raises money for research and treatment for neurofibromatosis (NF), a genetic disorder that causes tumors to grow in bones, nerves, and skin. The foundation acts as a coordinating body to link researchers, drug companies, and physicians who are working on NF to avoid duplication and share the latest information quickly.

Cupid's Undie Run is one of the principal sources of fund-raising. The tagline on their website is, "Cupid's Undie Run is where a little crazy meets a lot of charity. Tumors suck and we're here to fight them with the most fun event in the world. Join us on a mission you'll never forget!"

All the runners strip down to their "undies" and in Atlanta the course is roughly a mile around the Irby Avenue bar area, off Roswell Road. They also tout the pre- and post-parties as being the best fun in town. Last year, runners in 30 cities raised $2.8 million. This year, the foundation has already surpassed its goal of $3 million and money from the run is still coming in.

I told Mike and Kathryn that I would write a post about them and asked for photos. They sent me a couple, but they didn't send me any of them in their underwear. I probably should have asked them to do a reenactment by removing their clothes in the car and running around a parking lot. I guess there's always next year to photograph Mike and Kathryn.

For more information on the Children's Tumor Foundation, visit their website at http://www.ctf.org/.

Chapter 11
Oystering in Apalachicola Bay

Apalachicola is a quaint town on the Gulf coast of Florida that has the unofficial title of "Oyster Capitol of the World." It could once boast that most of the oysters in the U.S. came from Apalachicola Bay. However, many factors have contributed to reducing the harvestable oysters from the bay to a trickle. The recession also hit hard, but the downtown area has attracted new businesses and many of the homes that had fallen into disrepair are being restored. The town has diversified its economy by hosting art workshops, festivals, theater, and other events that attract participants, retirees, tourists, and people from nearby St. George Island.

Unfortunately, the town of East Point, where most of the oystermen live, has not fared as well. It was hit hard by Hurricane Dennis, but it is the lack of oysters that has struck the harshest blow. Much of the problem can be tied to water consumption in Atlanta and other towns along the Chattahoochee and Flint rivers. The reduced flow of the fresh river water into the bay has dramatically altered the ecosystem that allowed marine life and bird colonies to flourish.

On the beach side of one of the processing plants, I watched the oyster boats waiting their turns to come in and unload. The oysters are offloaded, and carried up to the shore where a forklift takes them up to the scale to be weighed where each oysterman is given a receipt. The bags are then stacked on pallets, iced-down, and loaded into a tractor trailer truck for shipment to South Florida. The *Tampa Bay Times* noted that in 2009, as many as 3 million pounds of oysters came from the bay. Now, it's a very small portion of that.

Most of the families in East Point have been oystering for generations. The man at right told me he had been oystering for 50 years.

I saw two men struggle with a burlap bag of oysters that they said probably weighed 200 lbs. Most of the bags I saw were much smaller, though, and I saw disappointment and despair on many of their faces. Oystering is hard work. The men use two long rakes, much like garden rakes, to bring the oysters to the surface. Once there, they sort them into those that can be harvested and those that have to thrown back because they are too small.

Recently, although the BP Oil spill didn't reach as far as the bay, about $4 million from the settlement will be used in a variety of ways to promote the recovery of Apalachicola Bay. However, it will not come soon enough to allow the oystermen of East Point to feed their families.

Be sure to visit the **Apalachicola Gallery** for more photographs of Apalachicola and East Point.

For more information on the current status of status of the bay area, go to **Apalachicola River Keeper**, a non-profit organization that monitors conditions in the water as well as the efforts to reshell the oyster beds.

Update: On a recent visit, my father told me that in 2015, only half as many oyster harvesting permits had been bought as in 2014. With the return of more tourists, some families are able to find low-paying jobs in the service industry. Many won't, however.

Chapter 12
Ronald Seaman: A Veteran's Surprising Recovery

Giving away two bottles of water during Dragon Con led to a conversation that would deepen my respect and appreciation for the veterans who have served our country and come home having sacrificed so much. That day, and in other conversations since then, Ronald Seaman, who is confined to a wheelchair, told me his story. He spent 25 years in the U.S. Army, and had spent three years in hospitals recovering from injuries incurred during his military service. He could not tell me any details because his missions were classified but he must have been grievously wounded to have spent so much time in hospitals He later alluded to having multiple surgeries and nerve damage. I met Seaman and his friend, Philip Shelton, who had also retired from the Army, during DragonCon. The convention is held in every Labor Day weekend. I had parked near a spot where a lot of characters were having professional photos taken, so I got out to wander around and to take some

pictures myself. I spotted a character in such an elaborate costume that I wanted to take a picture of, but he could move faster in a wheelchair than I could walk, so I thought I had missed my opportunity and headed back to my car.

Cosplay started in the U.S. early in the last century.

As the popularity of science fiction grew, it moved to Asia, where it came to prominence in the 1980s. Dragon Con, which is held every September in Atlanta, was launched in 1987, as a project of a local science fiction and gaming-group, the Dragon Alliance of Gamers and Role-Players (DAGR). Cosplay takes many forms and there are other conventions with overlapping programs. Enthusiasts often attend others such as **Comicon**, **Metrocon**, and **ShadoCon**. Typically, cosplayers dress and adopt the attitudes of characters in video games, comic books, movies, science fiction, fantasy, anime and other media. Many costumes rival any crafted in Hollywood. They are true works of art, with pain-staking attention to detail. The 3-4 day events usually include costume contests, parades, personal appearances from game companies, as well as characters or writers for television, movies, and literature. Dragon Con drew more than 57,000 people in 2013, and grows bigger every year. To

my surprise, when I got to my secret parking spot, there was the guy in the wheelchair and his friend who was helping him get the costume off. As I walked past, I told him that his costume was amazing. It was extraordinarily hot that day, and both men were sweat-soaked and looked exhausted.

I usually have bottled water in my car for Uber clients so I asked them if they would like some water. Both immediately said, "Yes," so I got some bottles from the car. While the three of us were getting rehydrated, I asked them how they came to know each other and how they had gotten into cosplay. Both said that they had retired from the military and were introduced through Seaman's daughter. Both liked science fiction and quickly became friends. Phillip said he was just the muscle behind the operation, helping Seaman get into and out of the costume and driving him to a couple of events. When we finished our water, I asked them if I could call them to interview them for my blog, and both agreed, giving me their cards.

After being released from the hospital, Seaman had severe vertigo, which pretty much confined him to bed. Knowing that his father could make most anything, and thinking that working with his hands would be good physical therapy, one of Seaman's sons suggested he try making cosplay costumes. Within just a few weeks, Seaman had fabricated a 6 foot Ironman costume and started working on costumes that fit over his wheelchair.

While he still had the vertigo, he quickly found that he could bear it as long as he was fabricating costumes, so he started to do some research and he set to work on another costume of his own design, but somewhat similar to those in one of the most popular video games ever, called *Gears of War*.

Seaman debuted the first costume at Metrocon, in Tampa, in 2013, and was mobbed, particularly by people who are fans of the video game. They were stunned by the complexity of the costume. He went to Comicon, in Tampa, the next month, and took second place in the costume contest. For Comicon, Seaman created a fictitious character, only loosely based on the video game, and titled himself, "Sergeant 1st Class, of the Handi-Capable Division. He couldn't figure out why everyone was calling him "Carmine."

He later realized that the costume was almost identical to that worn by a character named Clayton Carmine, in *Gears of War*, and that the judges had taken points off because the costume was not an exact replica of the one in the game.

In 2014, for Mega Con in Orlando, Seaman created another *Gears of War* costume similar to a Transformer, called a "Silver Back," and received "Judges Favorite" in the costume contest. One of the judges, Samantha Patrone, later borrowed a gun he had created for his Ironman suit.

After seeing him in the first two events, Seaman was quickly embraced by Dale Harvey and other members of the "26th RTI - The Unvanquished" cosplay group. They encouraged him and he has since fabricated costumes for others in the group. However, Seaman told me that he was especially grateful to F. Brian Mead, a noted cosplay fabricator, who has become his mentor and has taught him how to fabricate lighter, more versatile frames that put less wear and tear on his body.

He said that Mead and **Dale Harvey**, the founder of the group, had challenged him to create another

"Silver Back," similar to the one he had brought to Tampa and Atlanta. That particular costume is more than 6' tall and requires Seaman to navigate using a computer tablet mounted inside the suit that is connected to a Go-Pro camera incorporated into the outside design.

Harvey sent him a photo of the Silverback to use, and with advice from Mead, worked on building a structure that would fit on his new chair. He took the new to Palm Beach, Florida at Shadocon, last month, to rave reviews. Seaman's progress is evident on his Facebook page, and I have seen what a loving and supportive family he has. He and his wife, Barbara, have been married for thirty years, they have five children, and four grandchildren. They, too, must be lauded as we pay tribute to his service on behalf of his country. Families are truly the backbone of the U.S. military.

When I talked to him recently, Seaman said the he receives so much fan email that it's hard to keep up with all the people writing to encourage and praise for his designs. However, he told me that he has become much stronger since I last saw him and he is waiting anxiously for DragonCon in Atlanta over Labor Day weekend.

For him, the benefit of attending cosplay conventions is to meet other cosplayers. He not only creates new "builds," but works with other to design and fabricate their own costumes.

Seaman has become a sought-after motivational speaker and hopes his trans-formation may inspire other veterans who may be reluctant to take on new challenges. The Makers United for Children's Hope (MUCH) has become a vehicle for Seaman to impact the lives of children. Volunteer "Super Heroes" visit children who live with the restrictions of missing limbs, wheelchairs, or long hospital stays. Batman, Wonder Woman, Superman, Superwoman, Ghostbusters, Storm Troopers, Princess Leia, and other children's heroes visit the children and families, bringing gifts and hope to those who need it most.

A new effort of MUCH is providing customization of prosthetic limbs and wheelchairs based on the child's favorite super-hero. For example, here is a

Crystalheaven Photography

photo of a tricked-out wheelchair for a small Spider Man. Another, with a prosthetic limb, might choose an Ironman theme. Fabricators equip them with lights, sound, and secret compartments. As CEO, Zachary Hurst, told me, MUCH's goal is to provide something that a child wants to show off, rather than something that is seen as a limitation.

Hurst went on to say, "Working with your first prosthetic limb or operating within the restrictions of a wheelchair in day to day life can be a challenge for a well-adjusted adult. Imagine the world of a child living through the same experience. A child's world can, in some ways, be a crueler and more difficult place for adjusting to those changes."

I asked him about his new "Merman" costume that he recently debuted debuted. "How in the world can you get into that I'd be really claustropic, like I was in Spanx. If you don't know what those are, ask your wife," I quipped.

"Oh, I know exactly what they are. I had to learn to sew to create the costume. The back is made of stretch fabric, with a zipper."

Seaman has also started writing music and hopes to record his songs professionally. You can find some of them on **YouTube**. One of his recent songs is _**See You at the Next Con**_.

Sometimes we have defining moments in our lives that take us in directions we would never have considered. I am incredibly thankful for Seaman's service to protect us and inspired by his example of someone who found meaning and purpose when many would have given up. Seaman told me, "What I lost in the military I found with the 26th RTI. I hope I can inspire other veterans to take on new challenges. Sometimes It just takes getting over the fear of doing something new."

I would like to thank Dim Horizon Studios, MovinOverthemoon.com, Lawrence Munne, coyoteheaven.com, and anryDogStudios.com for the photos in the book. For more photos of Seaman's costumes and his design work, visit his new Facebook site Aracknoid3Cosplay or on my website www.talesfromundertheroof.com .

Chapter 13
Booze But No Boobs in ATL On Sundays

Sunday night I picked up a foursome in Virginia-Highlands, and could quickly tell that they had consumed a few too many adult beverages. A lively discussion ensued about their next port of call. Finally, they decided that they wanted to go to a strip club.

"Louise, "What is the closest strip club?"

Being an UberX driver, I didn't hesitate, replying, "The Clermont Lounge." This strip club, which has been open since 1965, boasts one of the most well-known exotic dancers, "Blondie." At age 57, she has been the subject of an independent film and is infamous for crushing beer cans between her breasts. I have also been told that couples' lap dances can be arranged. (I haven't seen any of this firsthand, by the way.)

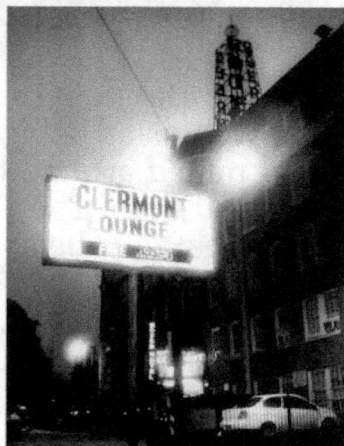

This would be easy, I thought. The Clermont was just around the corner. After a discussion about the merits of The Clermont, and other clubs like The Cheetah and Tattle Tales, the group decided on The Clermont, and off we went.

As we pulled up to the club, however, I could see that it was closed. *Oh no,* I thought, what now? Of course I knew the location of other clubs, but getting an agreement was going to be a challenge, because one of the women kept saying that buying a table at The Cheetah was $100. However, since it was the closest, the Cheetah won out, and off we sped.

In the meantime, I had Googled that club and their hours were listed as open "today" until 3:00 AM, However, when we got to The Cheetah, it, too, was closed, and the group decided that I MUST be at the wrong place. A lot of cursing ensued. One got out his smart phone and couldn't believe what he was seeing. He could see, but not believe, that the map showed us as being in the right location. Finally, as I pulled around to get out of the parking lot, I showed them The Cheetah's sign, and it was only then that they believed I did have some brain cells left.

At last, after I suggested that all the strip clubs might be closed on Sundays, and insisted that they call the next one on their list, we learned that they were closed, too. At first they wanted to go to a club in Buckhead, but after they realized the cost of the ride, they ended up by going back to the bar where I picked them up.

So, while you can drink and buy liquor on Sundays in Georgia, you can't get a lap dance except in the privacy of your own home.

Chapter 14
Christmas 1992

Although it does involve a car with a moon roof, it was a different car than I drive now. It was a beautiful car for the decades of the 1980s and 90s, a bright red Volvo station wagon with gold BBS wheels. Its turbocharged engine could make it fly. Uber was still 17 years away from inception and lighter-weight cell phones had just been introduced. My husband, Joe, was getting me a cell phone for Christmas, in fact.

Joe and I left Atlanta on Christmas Eve to spend the holidays with his sister, Frances, her husband, Alan, and their two daughters, in Murphy, North Carolina. Joe's dad was also with us.

Alan had been the pastor of the Presbyterian Church in Murphy for many years. Since their schedule made it hard for them to get away from home during the holidays, we typically drove to Murphy for Christmas.

The 1992 trip started the same way. With Joe's car too small, we drove my Volvo. I don't remember why we didn't leave Atlanta earlier, but given only a 3 hour trip, we didn't think anything of it. Just as we reached the mountains and it was inching toward dusk, however, I suddenly noticed that I had absolutely no response from the gas pedal. We were coasting.

Making a fast decision, I pulled off the four-lane highway in Cherry Log, Georgia, and coasted to a stop in front of a small house whose yard was full of junked cars and even the body of a school bus. It was also full of the typical things you might see throughout the rural South: wind chimes, a decorative well, birdhouses, heating oil tank, rusted farming equipment, and an old hot-water heater or two. The house was decorated with multi-colored Christmas lights and the windows were lit as well.

Given my self-described status of knowing everything about everything and wearing one of my many tacky Christmas sweaters, I thought I could solve the problem. Surely the car would restart and we would be on our way. However, none of my mojo worked, and there we were, stranded in Cherry Log on Christmas Eve. We knew Alan and Frances had church services that night, and it would be much later before we could reach them, so I begged Joe to go to the door of the house.

A portly man, about 60 years old, wearing overalls and a plaid shirt, came to the door. Hearing Joe's news, he invited the three of us in, and said he would call several mechanics who might try to come and diagnose the problem. Joe came back to the car to tell us, and we helped Joe's dad into the home.

However, as I started to enter, the cigarette smoke that came wafting out of the house nearly knocked me over. It would have been rude not to go in, but I knew that I would have a killer headache from the event.

I know this now, but at the time I didn't realize that almost all repairs to Volvos have to go to an authorized service center, and none of the man's calls to local shops were answered. Everyone had gone home to celebrate the holidays. It was very cold outside, and the family said we were welcome to stay just as long as we needed. We met the man's wife, who was in the kitchen cooking for relatives who were coming for dinner that night. Her hair was still in pink, fluffy hair rollers.

We were about an hour from Murphy, and with worship services not ending for another one, we did not expect to be rescued for a couple of hours. Rather than expose myself to second-hand smoke, and being a rude city girl, I decided that I would sit in the car. However, once in a while I had to go back inside to get warm. Joe and his father, more polite than I, stayed the course on the family's sofa.

As more and more of the family arrived carrying Tupperware containers, they would look at the two men sitting on the sofa and wonder what branch of the family they came from. They would say, "Hello," and scurry off to the kitchen to find out. (That was where the women were congregated.) Finally, Alan arrived to take us to Murphy and we left the keys to my car with the family who had welcomed us so warmly.

There are many advantages of having a minister in the family, and one is that they usually have people's home phone numbers. On Christmas Day, Alan called the local Ford dealer in Murphy, who put him in touch with a man who owned a car-hauler to get the Volvo back to Atlanta. I spoke to the man, and he couldn't do it the day after Christmas, but could do it the following one.

I was concerned about the cost, particularly since it would be about a 300 mile round-trip, so I asked, "How much do you usually charge to go to Atlanta."

"Well, I don't usually go to Atlanta," he responded.

"Well, how much would you charge for the trip; it's about 150 miles each way."

"Well," he responded, "I don't rightly know."

"Do you charge by the mile or by the time, or just how do you figure it out?"

"Well," I don't rightly know. Never been that far."

At this point, I couldn't think of any other way to ask the same question, so I gave up, assuming that I was looking at a $400-500 towing bill.

In subsequent calls to him and the family in Cherry Log the next day, we made the arrangements, and we used Alan's car to come back to Atlanta. Two days after Christmas, I met the car-hauler at the auto repair shop, and got a chance to meet him and his wife. Assuming that it was going to be several hundred dollars, I, asked, "Well, what do I owe you?"

He scratched his head, and finally answered my question. "Well," he said once again, "I reckon I'm gonna have to charge you $120.00." I could hardly believe this news and offered him my sincere thanks. I paid him in cash, and handed another $20 through the window, and I said, "Here, it's almost dinner time, why don't you take your wife out to dinner?"

"Why, thank you ma'am, we might just stop at the Cracker Barrel on the way home. I sure do appreciate it."

For a few years, we shared Christmas cards with the family in Cherry Log, but eventually we fell out of touch. I often think about that Christmas and what an impact the kindness of strangers can have.

Chapter 15
45th Annual Atlanta Pride Festival

Held on the second weekend of October to mark "Coming Out Day," the Atlanta Pride Celebration is one of the oldest in the U.S. Each year several hundred thousand gay men, lesbians, transgenders, and bisexuals, head to Atlanta to promote acceptance and equality. Uber drivers were on call throughout the 3-day event.

I didn't drive much of Pride Weekend because I was recovering from surgery. However, on Saturday night, I picked up two Uber clients at The Atlanta Eagle Club, across from Krispy Kreme Donuts. I was trying to justify sitting in the drive-through line behind at least 20 cars at the donut shop, when saved from a sugar overdose by the Uber beep. I called the clients to find out exactly where they were, and we quickly found each other. They were headed to a club on Cheshire Bridge Road.

The two of them were a contrast in appearance. The man in the front seat was conservatively dressed, wearing a plaid, button-down shirt, while the younger man, in the backseat, was dressed in leather. I quickly learned that they were brothers from North Carolina, and that the older one had invited the younger one to Atlanta for the weekend. For simplicity's sake, let's call the older brother, Jim, and the younger one, Perry.

Jim sat in the front, and Perry sat in the back. Jim started by apologizing for Perry, and it was apparent that while both had had a few adult beverages, Perry had had way too many. Jim then started berating his brother for embarrassing him in front of his friends and trashing his condo.

He turned around in his seat so that he could face Perry, and said, "I have paid all your expenses this weekend, and at the next place, I'm only buying you a soda. You have done nothing but embarrass me since you've been here. Why can't you just keep your mouth shut? And why can't you pick up after yourself? I walked into the brand new condo and your stuff was all over the place."

Jim continued, "Perry, Perry, you need to be quiet and listen to me. I want you to repeat what I'm saying. I want you to promise me that you won't embarrass me. If you don't behave, Papa Bear will have to send you home tomorrow. You know Papa Bear won't put up with this. Perry, I want you to repeat, 'If I don't behave and keep my mouth shut, Poppa Bear will send me home tomorrow.'"

This soon became a litany: apologies to me and exhortations to Perry. I felt bad for Perry because he was clearly past the point of repeating this or to make any lasting promises. I tried to change the subject but that didn't work, so I gave up after a couple of tries.

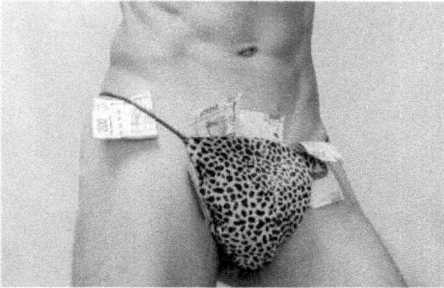

We pulled into the parking lot of their destination and Jim said, "This can't be right. This looks like a strip club." The three of us checked the sign and the address both matched, so Perry said he would go ask if we were in the right place. When he went to the entrance, the door opened and there stood a big hunk of a man wearing only a thong.

Jim immediately said to me, "Unh, uhn, we don't need to be here. This would be a big mistake. I think we need to get something to eat." I thought this was very astute and we found a nearby restaurant that was still open. It was largely deserted so I was pretty sure Jim wouldn't have to worry about Perry's behavior. I dropped them off and bid them adieu.

I hope I have learned a few things as I've aged. One is that there will always be friends or family who may not act as we might hope they would and we find ourselves feeling embarrassed. However, it is likely that others are more willing to accept these people than we are. It is sometimes hard, but we should try to love and embrace them as they are.

I have also learned that serious conversations are better held when both parties are sober.

Chapter 16
Larry the Lounge Lizard

I hadn't been driving for Uber very long and I got a call about midnight to pick up a client at a strip club, the Cheetah. My Uber client was standing in the parking lot, with a cell phone to his ear with his right hand, gesticulating wildly with his left. He was mid-forties, but was dressed as if trying to pass for a younger man in clothing fashionable perhaps a decade ago. He wore tight white jeans, a black shirt, and his bleached-blonde hair was tied back in the shortest ponytail I have ever seen. (I guess he didn't want hair to fall into his eyes and obstruct his vision during lap dances).

As an Uber driver, I pick up people all over the Atlanta area. Larry gave me a destination address that I input to Google Maps, however, the GPS program didn't list anything at that address, and he was he was back on the phone. I figured I would drive in that direction and try again as we got closer.

In the backseat, Larry was yelling at his girlfriend, who lives in Ottawa. He was obnoxious, rude, and very disrespectful of women. I knew what to expect. He accused her of being with another man, despite her contention that she was at a bar with her girlfriends.

He shouted, "I know you're out with another man you b*****. I hear men's voices in the background. You are such a f****** liar. I know you're cheating on me. You're nothing but a w****. I'm in my hotel room... I've been spending my frequent flier miles to see you and this is what you do to me, you go out and f*** someone else. I hope he f***s you good, but you will never find anyone who can f*** you as good as I can. I'm breaking up with you right now."

Meanwhile I was getting GPS directions that had me getting on and off I-285, which I knew were not right. I finally gestured at my client and told him that we were going around in circles. I apologized and offered to stop the Uber fare so that he wouldn't be charged. He insisted he had given me the correct address and hotel name.

Larry then started in on me, yelling at me about not being able to find the address, claiming that I was a terrible Uber driver, and said he would call the hotel and get directions. He called the hotel, started cursing at them, saying that they had given him the wrong address and he needed to know where the f*** the hotel was, and then hung up I thought he had gotten the address, but it turned out that they had hung up on him. He looked on their website and it had the same address. We were two for two. I wondered," Do other Uber drivers have to deal with this?"

Now, in his mind, we had suddenly become allies and we were driving around looking for the hotel. I knew it had to be nearby, but we couldn't spot it. Finally, just when I was about to give up, abandon him and my car, and call an Uber for myself, I was able to pull it up on MapQuest. In the end, it was on Galleria Parkway, just a mile or so away, and both Google Maps and the hotel's website were incorrect.

I was so relieved when I saw the hotel sign that I almost sang out, "Hallelujah, just get out of my f****** car." I was certainly thinking it. But he, too, was anxious to get out of the car because he had spotted a woman in the parking lot whom he knew.

He bolted out of the car, shouting to her, "Hey, where are you headed?" I couldn't hear her response but I could hear him shout, "Wait, I'll go with you."

If you pick up a guy at a strip club, he calls and berates his girlfriend, and then goes off with another woman he sees at the hotel, he's probably not good relationship material.

Chapter 17
How to Break Up a Fight While Driving

About 1:00 AM on a Saturday night, I got a fare in Virginia-Highlands. There were lots of people standing in the road, but one of the guys signaled that he was my passenger. I thought he was standing with a young woman but she didn't follow and he got in the passenger seat, up front, and we started the trip.

We had not gone very far and I could hear both sides of the conversation on his cell phone. I could hear a woman cursing and shouting at him, but he kept repeating the same refrain, "Do you want me to come back and get you?" I told him that would be OK with me, and after we were a few minutes into the ride, he asked me to turn around.

He got out of the car and went over to the woman and I could tell they were having a heated exchange. Finally, he got back in the passenger seat and she sat directly behind him in the backseat.

I never figured out what the argument was about, but she continued to shout and curse at him, and they argued about where they were going--his house or hers. All this time, he is saying to me, "She's my princess," over and over throughout the twenty-minute ride. She continued her tirade and then reached over into the front seat and tried to grab him around the neck.

At that point, I had to take action. What I really wanted to say was "Listen, b****, if you don't sit down and shut up, I'm going to put you're a**,out on Buford Highway and good luck on finding one out here at 2:00 AM." However, I just said, "Ma'am, you need to sit down and be quiet for the rest of the ride because I can't drive you safely."

She did stop, but she kept hitting the backseat with her fist. Throughout the fray, her companion just kept repeating, "She's my princess." Personally, I don't think the relationship will last.

Chapter 18
Across Continents and Years: Nigeria

As I related this story, a member of a writing group I attend, said, "How is it that you get such interesting people in YOUR car? Surely you must have some sort of record among Uber drivers." I, too, find it amazing that I encounter so many

Peter Onuh, Loretta Epuechi, and
Chukuemeka Ekpo

people whose lives have crossed mine in some way. Without Uber, I never would have continued to meet such fascinating and dedicated people.

In an earlier post, I wrote about meeting a man from Northern Sudan, whose life had been touched by a program I had been a part of 20 years ago. I certainly didn't expect that, nor did he. I was only one person who played a very small part of a massive effort, yet, here we were, in my car, headed to Atlanta's Buckhead bar area.

A few weeks ago, I got a call to pick up three Uber clients in downtown Atlanta. Someone else, who I think didn't even know them, used his Uber app to get them a ride to Atlantic Station.

Joni Lawrence

Earlier in the week, I had had dinner with a friend of 25 years, Joni Lawrence, the Associate Director of The Mectizan, Donation Program at the Task Force for Global Health in Atlanta. Joni frequently travels to African countries and we talked about surprising people when we can identify their home countries by recognizing African dialects, accents, and physical features. I wasn't surprised, therefore, when my Uber clients said they were from Abuja, Nigeria. I was, however, astonished, when they told me they were in Atlanta for a meeting at The Carter Center related to the Mectizan Donation Program. I had just started working at The Carter Center when this program was established.

Mectizan® is an anti-parasitic drug developed by Merck, a pharmaceutical company dating back to the 19th Century. The drug, whose primary component is Ivermectin, is used in the veterinary market in the U.S. for preventing certain parasites such as heartworms in dogs. In 1987, senior executives of Merck held a quiet meeting with Dr. William Foege, then executive director of The Carter Center, and another non-profit organization in Atlanta, now known as the Task Force for Global Health.

Bill Foege and Roy Vagelos on the 25th Anniversary

The visionary CEO of Merck, Roy Vagelos, said that the company had been looking for an anti-parasitic drug that could be used in humans, but Ivermectin was not effective in treating those most common in the U.S. He credits Mohammed Aziz, of Merck, with the idea that Ivermectin would be effective in treating onchocerciasis (River Blindness), however. Aziz had seen River Blindness cases when he had worked for the World Health Organization (WHO) in Eastern Africa and saw the drug's potential for prevention of the disease.

River Blindness is a disease prevalent in 36 Latin America and African countries and is transmitted by small black flies that congregate along fast-flowing rivers. When the flies bite, they transmit larva that then mate and produce worms that travel throughout the body. Adult females can release as many as 1,000 microfilariae per day in the human host. While there are many health conditions caused by the worms, the most serious is blindness, which occurs when the worms die and form scar tissue around the eyes. In endemic countries, it is common to see children leading the blind around with sticks.

As my husband, often reminds me, however, "The devil is in the details." Was there a way to ensure that the drug be given solely to humans, and not be diverted to the veterinary market where it would be used to prevent parasites in cattle and other animals? Given the lack of infrastructure in the affected countries and the prevalence of black markets, this would be an enormous challenge. Therein lay "the devil."

When interviewed by his alma mater, the University of Pennsylvania, in 1999, Dr. Vagelos said that he traveled the world for a year talking to governments and aid organizations before finding partners willing to take on this challenge. Its founding partners were The Carter Center and The Task Force for Global Health (TFGH).

Since 1987, many individual donors, governments, and aid organizations have joined forces and Ivermectin is now used not only to eliminate

River Blindness but also to prevent Lymphatic Filariasis.[10] This year marks the 25th anniversary of the program. The Carter Center estimates that more than 200 million treatments have been distributed by the partner organizations during this time. Columbia and Ecuador have been certified by the WHO to be free of the disease. In Uganda alone, The Center estimates that 2.7 million people have been saved from blindness.

Sir Emeka Offor, of Nigeria, shown here giving oral polio vaccine, contributed $250,000 to The Carter Center in 2013 for its efforts to eliminate river blindness in Nigeria, recently pledged additional monies to support distribution logistics. The Sir Emeka Offor Foundation is also a large contributor to other health and education programs in Nigeria as well as to Rotary International's Polio Eradication Program.

Of my new Nigerian friends, Peter Ekoja Onuh, is the programs officer of the Sir Emeka Offor Foundation. Loretta Epuechi and Chukwuemeka "Meka" Ekpo are public relations officers at the

---

[10] Lymphatic filariasis is a disease transmitted from person to person via mosquitoes. The adult worms live in the lymph system, where they reproduce, weakening the body's immune system.

Chrome Group, a regional conglomerate of oil and gas producers as well as other businesses of which Sir Emeka Offor is a member. The Group works closely with the foundation on the many health initiatives supported by the foundation.

Peter, Chukwuemeka, and Loretta were flying back to Nigeria the following day and wanted to

*Sir Emeka Offer and former President Jimmy Carter

make some last-minute purchases. I am proud to have met three of the people who are working so hard to eliminate river blindness and other preventable diseases.

Since this story was written, Sir Emeka Offer pledged another $10 million toward eliminating onchocerciasis in his country.

*Photos courtesy of The Mectizan Donation Program and The Chrome Group.

Chapter 19
Losing My Underwear in Europe

"Give us your tired, your poor, your huddled masses yearning to breathe free. The wretched refuse of your teaming shore." This is part of the poem composed by Emma Lazarus[11] to raise funds to build a base for the Statue of Liberty. My family has a similar approach when traveling to Europe. We leave our refuse behind. This was started by my father.

I have always had trouble with traveling "light." When we went to Egypt in 1995, I think we had seven pieces of luggage. Unfortunately, two were left behind in the airport, and even at that time, the airport was heavily guarded. Going through passport control, Joe had been detained in some room for 30 minutes because he had presented his military ID card.

It was a long flight, I was exhausted, Joe had been whisked away to god only knew where, and I was trying to get all of our luggage sorted out. As we reached our hotel, almost an hour's drive from the airport, I realized what I had done, and thought, *No problem, I'll just call the airline when we get to our hotel.* I never dreamed it would be so difficult.

---

[11] These words come from Lazarus' poem, *Collusus.* http://bit.ly/1s4ULfZ, accessed August 11, 2015.

Unfortunately, the airline office was only open the next time at 11 PM, and I would have to pick up my bags personally. Luckily we found a cab driver willing to take us back to the airport, but as an Egyptian citizen, he could not go into the airport--he could only take me so far. When we reached the airport, he got out and talked to the police for me and they agreed to help me find my two bags. Joe was not allowed to accompany me, either.

Suddenly I was surrounded by Egyptian soldiers wielding automatic weapons, and we started moving down innumerable steps into the bowels of the Cairo airport. Reaching the bottom, I could see a small cage, like a prison cell, and there were my two bags. None of the soldiers spoke any English I spoke no Arabic. They checked the numbers on the tags, I took the bags, and went back up the stairs carrying the luggage.

I rendezvoued with Joe and the taxi driver. By the time we got back to our hotel, it was well after midnight and we had a 7 AM wake up call to start our tour.

Since then, I have pared my list of travel essentials considerably. For this trip to Europe, having a cracked sternum, I insisted we go out and buy "light" luggage. We were able to cram everything into one large and one carry-on bag (that we checked). A backpack held my computer tablet, as well as "plane reading."

I wish I could say that I came up with two other strategies that has helped reduce our essentials on my own, but I have to credit my parents for two of them. My mother, Elizabeth, takes a loop of string and hat pins, creating a mini-

clothesline where she can hang her hand-washed underwear to dry. My father, Billy, takes his oldest underwear, and just throws it away.

I decided to try my father's approach this year. I packed my oldest panties and bras, and discarded several of them in England. Joe packed an extensive magazine collection and threw them away as he read them.

When we went to the Victoria and Albert Museum in London, there was a special exhibit on fashion in the United Kingdom during World War II, when everything had to be rationed. In fact, for most things, it lasted until 1949. The exhibit had many patterns and examples of how to make old clothes more stylish changing buttons, adding a bow, or turning a man's suit into a dress. If my underwear in London is found by someone who lived during that time, they could take the lace around the top of one pair of panties and turn it into a lace collar.

When I thought about it further, however, I realized that my father's discarded underwear probably weighs, at most 1/2 pound. Joe's magazines and books seemed to be the best idea until yesterday, when he came running for the bus in a little town in France carrying a heavy wooden bowl. Even if we left all of our underwear in Europe, I didn't think it would equal the weight of the bowl. However, it will provide many memories of our trip and the airlines will be happy to take our money for one more bag.

On a recent trip to see my parents, I learned that my father not only left his underwear, but most of his clothes. He gave them to one of the cabin stewards. Next time, I'll be ready.

Chapter 20
My Underwear Confession

OK, I admit it. While I did throw underwear away on my recent trip to Europe, I also had to buy some new things to go under my chosen attire. Here's that side of the story.

Since I retired, I can usually be found in my pajamas or skirted leggings (as if I'm just on my way to yoga). For this trip, I assumed that London could be chilly, so I packed several lightweight sweaters and I wore the same black "broomstick" skirt for three days, with different tops. It was so cold, however, I had to buy a heavy sweater. I bought it in part because the woman in the market stall had a sign reading, "Retiring, everything 20% off." It has big shoulder pads and makes me look like I should be in the *Nine to Five* movies, with a big, bouffant hairstyle.

For the Riveria, I assumed that it would be warm, but the lightweight sweaters might be good for hiding the baggy skin under my arms. I bought a couple of midi-dresses because they are comfortable and can be dressed up or down. I figured they were a good hybrid of style and comfort.

Next was the questions of undergarments. For several years, I have been looking for Flexees body briefers, sort of like babies' onesies. They were lightweight and smoothed over the tire around my middle. Mine, however, were threadbare, so I finally had to take the plunge and try to find something else.

Since the advent of Spanx, it has become impossible to buy just one undergarment; you have to buy each piece separately and there are even videos on how to choose what one "needs" to smooth those "problem areas." Did you see Tina Fey on *David Letterman*? She was wearing several Spanx-like garments that smooth the waist and thighs, but there's a cutout in the front so that you can wear your own bra. What sense does this make?

Instead of having two straps over your shoulders, now you have four to adjust. In addition to the "over the stomach" briefer, she was wearing control-top pantyhose. How do you go to the bathroom in this getup? I don't even want to think about that. One

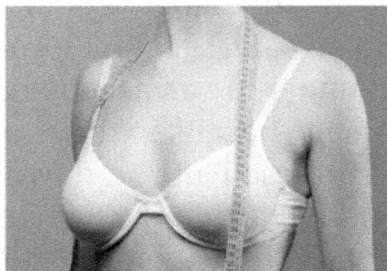

woman on a recent trip shared a quip that instead of measuring the height of their children, some women keep a tape measure on the back of the bathroom door to see when and how far their breasts have gotten lower as they have gotten older.

I think women have been lured into thinking that we could confine everything into one more or less sleek look from head to toe, with Spanx going down to our ankles. Everything seems designed to force skin, bones, and organs into the tiniest of spaces. Of, if you wanted, you could buy padded bras to emphasize the "girls," or padded panties for a big-butt look.

I have earned my wrinkles and my cellulite, and all I wanted was something simple like the Flexees that would lift the "girls" into an approximation of their former location and smooth over the extra skin around my waist.

I finally elected to try two knee-length, stretch slips that I knew I would be pulling down constantly, two medium-weight bodysuits with built-bras a cup size too large (because they don't make my size), and two body briefers without built-in bras. For the latter, I thought I could just push the "girls" into one area 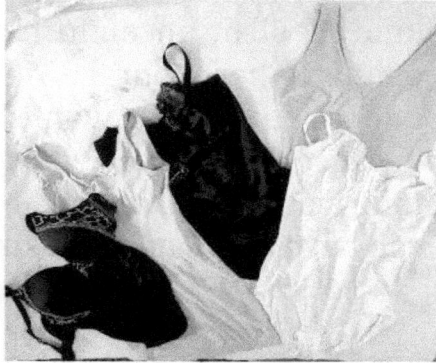 and hope that they wouldn't move downward as the day progressed. I tried everything on again when I got home and, while not ideal, I thought they were workable.

The first day I wore one of the body briefers, I had been wearing it all day, and I felt that my panties were not only in a wad, but cutting me in half at the same time. It was our first day on a cruise, and I had to get out of it. The problem was that our main luggage had not arrived yet, so I couldn't leave the room "camo style." Then I realized that I hadn't thought of finding panties to go under the body-sculpting slips. So...I'll let you guess which option I finally chose: 1. Adult disposable panties, or 2. Joe's white boxer shorts. (Just don't tell Joe.)

Why do we feel we need to emulate television or movie personalities who don't even look like they do in real life? I think Tina Fey is one of the funniest and most creative people alive. Next time I try to talk myself into buying something that I know I will be uncomfortable wearing, I hope I can emulate her courage in showing people the underside of what women will do to themselves because we are exposed to a barrage of information that we can be "better, more beautiful, can have it all," and you know the rest.

Chapter 21
Martin Luther King, Jr. and I
Selma, Alabama 1965

I asked one of my Uber clients on the King Holiday if she had seen the movie, *Selma.* She said, "Yes, I found it very powerful."

Then I asked, "So, does the movie focus primarily on Dr. King, or does it feature people like Amelia Boynton, and the many other local organizers?"

She hesitated and then said, "Well, it focused primarily on Dr. King, but there are references to others who helped and organized the demonstrations there."

I don't think I can see the movie. Or at least, I will wait until it comes out on DVD and I can watch it at home. It's not because I do not support the continuation of Dr. King's work, but because one of the most powerful moments in my life occurred as the result of the Selma campaign and gave me a unique perspective on Dr. King's life as well as those who put their lives on the line to further the goals of the civil rights movement. Seeing the movie in a theater might prove too difficult for me emotionally.

I was only 12 years old in 1965, and while my parents, in the minority of all of our white, Southern Baptist neighbors, supported the aims of the Civil

Rights Movement, I don't really remember seeing the Selma campaign on television. My father owned a business in Atlanta, right around the corner from Ebenezer Baptist Church, so I was in the neighborhood all the time. In addition, the City of Atlanta business leaders, after the early student protests downtown, had decided that Atlanta would not be a Birmingham, also known as "Bombingham." We, therefore, did not have the level of civil rights activity on the streets. Ours occurred largely behind closed doors.

My intersection with Selma came some 12 years later, after I had gotten out of college. I worked for a year at the Atlanta History Center, and then applied for a position at The King Center to help process the records of many of the civil rights organizations that had been collected by an earlier project. The project was funded by the National Endowment for the Humanities and the principal on the grant was a professor at the University of South Carolina, Dr. Willie L. Harriford.

After a few weeks, I called to check on the progress of the hiring, and to my surprise, without even an interview, I was told that I had been selected as one of the two assistant archivists. The salary was almost twice what I was making, so I was elated. As a young, naïve, and somewhat ignorant white woman of twenty-three, I really had no idea what a turning point that would be in my life.

I was the first person hired, so I showed up at The King Center, ready to work, only to find that no one was expecting me. At that time, The King Center operated from the basement of the Interdenominational Theological Seminary, on the Atlanta University complex. The archives, with all the of papers from the Southern Christian Leadership Committee (SCLC), the Student Nonviolent Coordinating Committee (SNCC) and many other organizations, were housed in a protective cage in boxes normally used in archives.

Over the next few years, there was a high turnover rate and I eventually found myself responsible for the archives, and later the museum and started the multi-volume, *King Papers Project.*[12] The archives moved to the newly-completed complex on Auburn Avenue, in 1981-1982. During the five years between when I held the position, several scholars were working on books about Dr. King, and anxiously awaited the opening of the archives that occurred in October 1981.

Meanwhile, I was trying to make sense of Dr. King's speeches, sermons, recordings, and documents of the SCLC. One of the things that made it challenging was that Dr. King had sent a

[12] Carson, Clayborne, ed., *The Papers of Martin Luther King, Jr.* (Berkeley and San Francisco: University of California Press,).

large number of his papers to Boston University and there was another group at Mrs. King's home on Sunset Avenue, in addition to those at The King Center.

As I worked, I felt I came to know Dr. King and many of his associates: James Orange, James and Diane Bevel, Andrew J. Young, Hosea Williams, Bernard Lafayette, Jr. and John Lewis, to name only a small few. David Garrow, author of *Protest of Selma,*[13] had petitioned for release of the FBI papers under the Freedom of Information Act, while writing a biography of Dr. King, and was collecting and sharing documents that he found from other sources.

Stoney Cooks, who also worked at The King Center, was trying to identify film and audio files of Dr. King's speeches and sermons. Cynthia Lewis came on board during this time, as well. So many things were scattered and undated that we had to collaborate closely to pin down dates and places. I met frequently with Mrs. King, and since The King Center had such a small staff, we were all called upon to accept roles we never imagined as the national park and the first holiday were celebrated.

Mrs. King told me that she had had a professional appraiser come in to set a value on The King Papers. "They told me there was no value

---

[13] Garrow, David J., *Protest at Selma: Martin Luther King, Jr. and the Voting Rights Act of 1965,* (Yale University Press, 1978).

in the papers because so much was done over the phone." She would always go on to say, however, "I don't believe this; the papers are the only legacy I can leave to my children. I think the appraisers are wrong." Ironically, even those phone recordings would eventually come to light with the release of the transcripts of the phone conversations on phones the FBI was monitoring, she would be proved correct on the initial appraisal.

My personal transformation came on an ordinary day, going through box after box of documents. Of course I had read King's *Letter from the Birmingham Jail,* but I was told that notes for that letter had been written on toilet paper and small bits of paper smuggled in and out of the jail in Birmingham. Those were likely scattered in private hands, and would not be easily surrendered.

One day, after sifting through many pro forma letters, and routine office memoranda, I found a document that I didn't expect. It was written on Waldorf Astoria Hotel stationery, where Dr. King had stayed in New York after receiving the Nobel Peace Prize. I recognized his hand-writing right away. I also recognized that of Andrew Young. If I remember correctly, it was not dated nor did it have a title.

It had not been referenced in Garrow's book,[14] because the archives had not yet opened to scholars. Based on the stationery and the document's content, I suspected that this was written by King while he was in jail in Selma, February 1-5, 1965. There were twelve directives to Andrew Young, who was allowed to visit King and Ralph David Abernathy during their pre-planned incarceration. Garrow, who was working on his the Pulitzer-Prize winning book, *Bearing the Cross: Martin Luther King, Jr. and the Southern Christian Leadership Conference,*[15] and I conferred and decided that it must have been written on February 2, 1965.

As Garrow would later point out,[16] this document represented a strategic change in the way pressure would be brought to bear on President Lyndon Johnson and Congress to pass the Voting Rights Act. Rather than withdraw to Atlanta, while local leaders continued the protests, King and the SCLC would maintain a significant presence in Selma. King admonished Young, "Let me hear...on all of this tomorrow morning."[17]

By this time, I had handled many of Dr. King's handwritten drafts of speeches and sermons, and I was the custodian of his briefcase and Nobel Peace Prize, but my relationship with the man

---

[14] Garrow, *Op. cit.*
[15] Garrow David J., *Bearing the Cross: Martin Luther King, Jr. and the Southern Christian Leadership Conference* (New York: William Morrow & Co., 1986).
[16]*Ibid,*
[17] *Ibid.*

himself was still distant. In addition, I had not seen other documents that demonstrated the level of Dr. King's day-to-day role in shaping the agenda of the civil rights movement. I had seen the side he presented in public events--as a stirring orator, a spiritual leader, and a figurehead.

I can't tell you why this document, in particular, made such an impact on me, but it did. From that time on, I had a greater respect and appreciation of Dr. King and I felt overwhelmed that I would have the singular honor of caring for his papers. I also felt a duty to make sure his papers were united, in one place, which would be open to scholars and the documents would be displayed for the public.

When I left The King Center in 1987, I worried that the precarious funding of the organization might result in the papers languishing in the archives under uncertain circumstances and unavailable to scholars such as Taylor Branch, who went on to write the definitive trilogy of books about America in the King Years, one of which also won the Pulitzer Prize.[18]

I would hear disturbing reports of a leaky roof over the archives at The King Center, lack of access, disagreement among Dr. King's heirs, and other things that left me feeling that there was little hope that the papers, as well as Dr. King's

---

[18] Branch, Taylor, *America in the King Years* (New York: Simon & Schuster, 1988-2006).

home library and the papers remaining there, would ever be brought together and be properly curated. It disturbed me greatly and would do so for more than 20 years. I admire Dr. Clayborne Carson, the editor of The King Papers, for his perseverance in continuing that effort throughout the tumultuous decades.

While I was aghast that King's heirs would ask for and receive a whopping $37 million for the purchase of the papers, in 2007, I was hopeful. I still worried, however, that because former Mayor Shirley Franklin's consortium had had to spend so much money on buying the collection, it would be difficult to raise additional funding for its preservation and a facility in which it would be properly preserved and displayed. The continuing fight among Dr. King's surviving children over his Nobel Peace Prize and travel Bible, appalls me.

On the King Holiday, when WABE 90.1 FM aired an interview with Doug Shipman, the CEO of the Civil and Human Rights Musem, talking about displaying some of the Selma documents penned in King's hand, I felt a burden had been lifted from my shoulders. While it was a weight on my spirit that no one asked me to assume, it had been there, nevertheless. Sometimes I go and sit by Dr. King's tomb in quiet reflection. The next time I go, it will be in respectful celebration.

Chapter 22
Sex in France: Juste une minute s'il vous
Or, you can get it 24/7

The French have been lauded for their wine, food, and some would say, their antipathy toward Americans. There's also a lot of buzz about the French and sex. As a teenager, I swooned over Jean-Claude Killy, the triple gold-medal Olympic skier. None of my girlfriends knew the correct pronunciation of the French in the Beatles' song, "Michelle," but we certainly longed for a boy to write a song like that for us. We could hardly wait for the meeting of the Camp Fire Girls to be over so that we could play music, toss our hair over our shoulders, and dance. In fact, we saw the Beatles perform at Atlanta Stadium in 1965.

As an American in France, on the Riveria no less, I was curious. *Is it true that the French have more sex, or better sex? Do they even have sex? Knowing only bonjour, sortie (which is very important if you want to find the exit from the metro station), merci, and toilette, I was at a loss. Oh, and I almost forgot, I know the French term, ménage à trois, but I didn't think my husband would go for that.*

While pondering these questions, I pretended to be a cultured and polite American tourist, visiting three Medieval towns high in the hills above Nice. The French don't speak English, of course but they all know the acronym "ATM." While getting more Euros, I spotted something I'd never seen outside of a bathroom: a condom dispenser. It was hanging right there on a medieval wall in Tourrettes-sur-Luop. *Interesting juxtaposition,* I thought. *Modern art,* I wondered. After all, many of the 2,400 people living there are artisans, and many well-known artists such as Marc Chagall and Pablo Picasso spent time there and in the nearby village St.-Paul-de-Vence.

Perhaps I could demonstrate my sophisticated appreciation of modern art by buying it, I thought, but I couldn't find a price tag, only a slot for accepting money.

 Having a machine out in the open, however, struck me as odd. After all, in such a small town, everyone probably knows everyone else's business. Wouldn't you at least want the privacy of a pharmacy? Not knowing how to ask why they had a condom machine on a medieval wall, however, I couldn't ascertain the answer. You may notice a pattern in a few photos I took. There are no people around. Maybe it's true. Perhaps they're all inside having sex, I thought.

The next town on our itinerary, St.-Paul-de-Vence, was much bigger, and had so much to see, that I forgot to look for prophylactics. On the last day of our trip, however, in the old part of Nice, France, I spotted another condom machine, this time a much larger one with more options. It was just outside the doors of a pharmacie (in the French spelling). It was also near the flower and vegetable market, as well as popular tourist attractions that many people visit. In the mornings, in particular, the large tourist boats anchor nearby and have shore excursions.

Hmmm, what could explain this phenomenon, I wondered. And then it hit me! The condom machines were probably not for French residents, but rather for the tourists. The medieval hill towns above Nice are popular with cyclists, hikers, and tourists of all ages. I remembered seeing a bus full of college-age students unload at one of the villages, and suspected that they were spending a summer abroad or at least on some supervised trip.

Placing condom dispensers next to the ATM and the pharmacie was brilliant. What teacher or some tourist hoping to "get lucky" with a companion that night would question a quick trip to the ATM or to the pharmacie? If they didn't speak French it might be a time-consuming or embarrassing affair. However, the dispensers are clearly marked and you just put your Euros in the slot under the ones you think best, and voilà, you're ready for whatever might come your way-- unless, of course, you need Viagra or some other prescription medication.

Back in the U.S. now, I am still in a quandary. So what is the truth about the French and sex? I don't even know whether my hypothesis is correct. I think I need to go back to France and stake the condom machines out. Whenever someone buys from the machine, I could run over and ask if they speak French and why they are using them. Or, maybe not such a good idea.

If any of you have answers, please let me know. That way I can cross this question off my list.

Chapter 23
Honoring Our Georgia Veterans

My husband, Joe, asked me to go with him to the memorial honoring the forty-two members of the Georgia Army National Guard (GARNG) who died in the "war on terrorism." It's on the grounds of the new headquarters for the Guard, which is named for General Lucius Clay, who led the Berlin Airlift in 1948.[19] On Saturday, the Dobbins Air Reserve Base (DARB) was almost deserted and we were the only visitors at the site.

The National Guard memorial is under the shade of a centuries-old oak tree, a very tranquil and peaceful space. The design includes plaques with photos of the victims, as well as their rank

---

[19] The Berlin Airlift, 1948-1949, supplied food, medicine, fuel and other supplies to West Berliners after the Soviets blockaded train and road supply routes into the city. The airlift by allied forces succeeded in keeping West Berlin from falling under Soviet rule. http://www.history.com/topics/cold-war/berlin-airlift Accessed July 6, 2015.

and date of death. In the middle of the wall is a small fountain that adds a soothing effect. It was dedicated on August 7, 2014, and Joe had not had an opportunity to see it since it was finished. As a

part of the fund-raising effort, service members could buy bricks that form the pathway, and Joe had bought one. Beginning in 2003, approximately two-thirds of the Georgia Army National Guard personnel were called to active duty and deployed overseas.

Joe chose to attend North Georgia College because of its ROTC program. He had enjoyed scouting, achieving Eagle Scout rank, and thought he might want a career in the military. He was commissioned in the U.S. Army upon graduation. He served for three years in what was then West Germany before being discharged and assigned to the Inactive Ready Reserve. In 1985, he went to work for the Georgia Army National Guard, at Dobbins, and joined the 151st Military Intelligence Battalion, as a guardsman.

He went on to serve in many fields within the guard, including in a MASH[20] unit. After 9/11 he moved to the guard's state headquarters, working with GEMA[21] in the field of emergency preparedness. His work there led to another promotion and a return to Dobbins. He spent the last 11 years of his thirty-year career in that field before retiring from the military in 2010.

Our next stop was the small white chapel across the street from the memorial. Joe has always been a history buff, so he knew something about its origins. "The chapel building itself dates from around 1942 it was built by a company in North Carolina and shipped, in pieces, to Europe during World War II. I think it was used on an air base there, and then returned to the U.S. after the war." There were a number of American air bases used in the strategic bombing campaign against Germany."

The Dobbins Chapel was returned to North Carolina after the war and was deemed "army surplus." The Georgia Department of Defense

---

[20] Mobile Army Surgical Hospital
[21] Georgia Emergency Management Agency

website[22] indicates that it was moved to Marietta in 1949 by volunteers from the 116th Fighter Group Wing, and reassembled near the main gate of the air base.

"Most of the chapels from this era fell into disrepair and were eventually demolished, Joe recalled. I remember attending a memorial service in the Dobbins chapel, in 1987, for a pilot who had died in a crash. It, too, was in such bad shape that it was about to be torn down. However, a group of WWII veterans who remembered the chapel when it was overseas, lobbied to save it, and helped raise money for its restoration." In 2012, a similar group of angels stepped in, raising the money to move the chapel down the air base runway to the grounds of the GNARD.[23]

---

[22] http://www.gadod.net/command-updates Accessed June 7, 2015.

[23]http://www.gadod.net/command-updates Accessed June 7, 2015. Other photos of the chapel may be found at http://bit.ly/1RWDgLb

CHAPTER 24
Louise and Joe's Big Adventure, 2015
The Grand Prix of Monaco

Joe and I have travelled to many countries. Happenstance sometimes leads us in unplanned directions. Last year, for example, we went to Russia, going from Moscow to St. Petersburg on a river cruise. Being able to talk to people was one of the highlights of our trip. My parents, who had been twice, told us what to expect. Our companions were quite surprised by the beauty of the country and the warmth of the Russian people.

I received an email about an English travel package to France and Italy, with tickets for the Grand Prix of Monaco. Sports car racing is in my DNA, but I had never been to a Formula 1 race. Much to my surprise, Joe really wanted to go, so we changed our plan to see Greece and Turkey.

We spent four days in London, in a flat I found on Airbnb.com. Museums and restaurants were high on our list of activities, and as usual, we saw as much as possible. Then it was on to Nice, France, for two days. The highlight of our time there was spent visiting three medieval towns: Tourettes-Sur-Loop, St. Paul de Vence, and Gourdon (shown above). Each had been a fortress, perched high on mountain tops, in the Middle Ages, like the town of Over the years, the beauty of the area attracted

other artists like Pablo Picasso and Marc Chagall. St. Paul de Vence, where the Chagalls built a home, is the largest. The fortress was erected in the 1400s and can only be entered through one of two entryways.

St. Paul, shown below, features breath-taking views of the hills around Nice, all the way to the sea. The town is the home of many artisans and

one has to look closely in order to see art tucked in nooks and crannies. Even the path throughout the village is made of cobble-stones in the shape of flowers. We left our tour group and rode the bus back to Nice after an afternoon spent wandering into shops and galleries.

The next day we boarded a ship that took us to the Italian town of Livorno, and the French cities of Cannes, and St. Tropez.

The highlight of our trip was the Formula 1 race in Monte Carlo, however. We had grandstand seats facing the harbor, where yachts packed full of people anchored. Behind us, spectators filled every mountainside balcony.

Racing on the streets of the exquisite crown jewel of Monte Carlo began in 1929. With the exception of the war years, the race has been run each year. It is considered the highlight of the Formula 1 season, in part because it is the only race still run on city streets. All of the other events are held at race tracks around the world.

Many of our travel companions were from England, there to cheer for Lewis Hamilton, (shown here) the British native and favorite to win. He has dominated the sport, driving at a very young age, with world championship wins in 2008 and 2014. This race was special to him because he now lives in Monaco. He needed a win there.

The Monte Carlo circuit is challenging, even for the most experienced drivers. Not only does it include a tunnel under a waterfront hotel, the course rises from the harbor, up and down the steep terrain to and from the famous casino and the Hotel de Paris. It is 2.074 miles long and has 19 turns. It has the slowest turn of any circuit, at 30 mph, but speeds on the straight-aways can rise to 160 mph.

The city's narrow streets make it difficult to overtake and pass other cars. Under these conditions, it is the driver's skill that matters most. Over the 78 laps, drivers make more than 4,000 gear changes. Safety is a serious concern, and it is unlikely that the course would meet today's standards. Its history, however, keeps it on the Formula 1 circuit.

The day was beautiful with a bright blue cloudless sky. The azure waters of the Mediterranean sparkled. The temperature climbed into the 80s, so many of the British abandoned the grandstands for an air-conditioned bar and a big-screen television.

Everyone watched from the grandstands, waiting impatiently to cheer Hamilton on as he went under the bridge into view as he approached the "swimming pool" turns where we sat. Jumbotrons allowed us to see him take the lead on the first lap. In second and third were his Mercedes teammate, Nico Rosberg, and the Ferrari driver, Sebastian Vettel.

On the 64th lap, with only 14 laps remaining, Max Verstappen, in the Toro Rosso Renault, crashed into

Lotus driver Romain Grosjean, sending the tires of the Toro Rosso flying off and leaving the car firmly stuck in the safety barriers on turn1. Typically, the corner workers get the driver to safety and clear the accident quickly, using a crane to get the car off the track.

While Verstappen was okay, the car was so deeply embedded, officials had to deploy the "virtual safety

car." Drivers are signaled to slow down by using yellow "safety" lights deployed around the track. However, as removal efforts continued, they had to send the safety car, shown here, to further protect the corner workers desperately trying to remove the damaged car.

Hamilton led the race from the beginning. However, cloudy and cool temperatures on previous days prevented the drivers and technicians from evaluating tire performance under race conditions. Formula 1 cars use "slick" tires that maximize contact with the track surface by eliminating the grooves found on conventional tires. At higher speeds, on a hot track, tires degrade more quickly. This would prove critical to the outcome of the race.

Many teams use these delays to bring the car into the pits for tire changes or other small adjustments. The reduced speeds have a significant impact on the tires because they become cooler and create less traction. In addition, temperature changes caused by slower speeds can impact the integrity of the tires. On safety laps, drivers must maintain their positions, unable to pass other cars.

Hamilton radioed Paddy Lowe, the chief engineer, asking if he should come in for tires. He assumed that the second and third place cars would do so as well. He could see their positions on the Jumbo-trons and, with a 21 second lead, he thought he would have time.

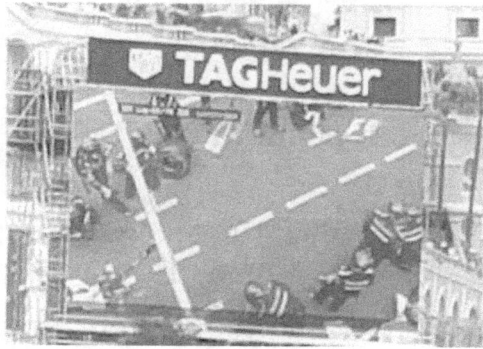

As he moved toward the pit entrance, the Mercedes engineers frantically crunched the numbers, taking into account the lead, the speed of the cars behind the safety car, and how long the pit stop would take. Could they get him in and out in time to exit in the lead position. The crewed stood ready in the Mercedes pit, shown above, to change the tires. Just a few hundred feet from the pit entry, they radioed Hamilton to come in. The actual tire change can take as little as four seconds.

As he went back onto the track, however, Hamilton realized that had lost the number one position. He

exited behind Rosberg, and beside Vettel. (Shown above)

He radioed the Mercedes engineer, "I've just lost this race, haven't I?"[24]

Pulling into third position, behind Vettel and Rosberg, Hamilton waited for racing to be resumed.

One can only imagine Hamilton's disappointment and frustration. Human error had led to the discrepancy in timing, and neither Vittel nor Rosberg had pitted.

---

[24] The Daily Telegraph. *Hamilton Counting Cost of Blunder*, page B15. London:May 25, 2015.

The safety car was removed on Lap 70 and racing continued. However, with only eight laps remaining, Hamilton could not overtake and pass the the Ferrari or the other Mercedes. When the checkered flag came out, there were audible gasps throughout the crowd. Hamilton came in third, just 1.5 seconds behind Vettel's Ferrari, and 6.05 seconds from his teammate at Mercedes, Rosberg.[25]

While Joe and I continued our trip, Hamilton remained sequestered in his apartment. He still led in overall points, but he would have to rely on his driving skills as well as the car's performance to win the 2015 Formula 1 championship.

Race photos used with permission of the photographer, Luka Radek.

---

[25]Ibid.

CHAPTER 25
Stimulant Use on Campuses

I rarely pick up the same client twice, however, I have driven 'Bryan' twice. The first time I met him, he had been at law school for only a few days. He was somewhat embarrassed to admit that he was going only to buy cigarettes. We chatted, stopped for cigarettes, and I took him back to campus the second time, he remembered me, remarking, "I've ridden with you before. "You picked me up to buy cigarettes. I was really embarrassed."

"Oh, I remember now. How are things going," I asked. "I don't judge people—everyone has their vices."

"All the students are nervous about exams that are starting next week. All the students in the law school are going to the doctor--getting prescriptions for Adderall or Ritalin--to help them get everything done and prepare for exams.

Brian told me his strategy was to get up at 6:00 AM, take a pill, study until 2:00 PM, take a break, and then study until 2:00 AM. In order to stay on this regimen, his strategy is to leave the pill bottle and a glass of water on his nightstand. "That way," he assured me, "When the alarm goes off at 6:00 AM, I won't roll over and go back to sleep.

My passenger also told me that he had a plan to stop smoking--right after exams-- but he was worried about his ability to stick with it. "I'm going to a big wedding where there will be a lot of smokers, and then at Christmas I will be with Albanian members of my family, all of whom smoke. I'm just not sure that I won't be tempted."

"I'm sure you'll try and if you don't succeed, you can always try again."

Given Brian's report on stimulant use during exams, I decided to take an informal, unscientific, poll of students who pinged me for Uber as well as students I met elsewhere.

The results of my poll were surprising. The majority of my sources intimated stimulant usage is high among undergraduates and graduate students.

There was only one exception. Three business school graduate students just laughed when I questioned them. "We don't worry about exams because the business school doesn't grade the same way and we don't have finals. That's why we can go out partying tonight," the first one said. When I picked up his two fellow However, I have since learned that the abuse of stimulants like Adderrall and Ritalin is extremely high in schools, including adolescents in grades eight to twelve.

Stimulants are approved for children and adults who suffer from attention-deficit hyperactivity disorder (ADHD) In this cohort, the stimulant..."often in conjunction with cognitive therapy, helps to improve ADHD symptoms along with the patient's self-esteem, thinking ability, and social and family interactions." The students I questioned—who did not have ADHD—told me they use the drugs to hyper-focus on writing papers, taking exams, and studying. They also said that they were readily available on campuses without a prescription.

The National Institute on Drug Abuse, however, reports, "...stimulants do promote wakefulness, but studies have found that they do not enhance learning or thinking ability when taken by people who do not actually have ADHD. Also, research has shown that students who abuse prescription stimulants actually have lower GPAs in high school and college than those who don't.

For more information, visit the NIDA website:www.drugabuse.gov.

ABOUT THE AUTHOR

Louise Cook is an Atlanta native who lives in Decatur. She has always been an avid reader and her career required a great deal of academic and professional writing. Taking her love of words in another direction, she authored this book and is writing stories about her extended family and friends, most of whom share a passion for fast cars, loud engines, and laughter.

She publishes a blog, Tales From Under The Moon Roof, about the people she meets while driving for Uber (a ride-sharing company), friends, family, and current events. She and her husband love to travel, and she posts from whatever road she's on, collecting stories as she makes new friends and finds new places to explore.

For more information, visit her website:

www.talesfromunderthemoonroof.com

www.ingramcontent.com/pod-product-compliance
Lightning Source LLC
LaVergne TN
LVHW021350080426
835508LV00020B/2211